EXPERIENCING
the TRUTH

EXPERIENCING
the TRUTH

Bringing the Reformation
to the African-American Church

ANTHONY J. CARTER, KENNETH JONES,
AND MICHAEL LEACH

Edited by Anthony J. Carter

CROSSWAY BOOKS

WHEATON, ILLINOIS

Published by Crossway Books
a publishing ministry of Good News Publishers
1300 Crescent Street
Wheaton, Illinois 60187

Design and typesetting by Lakeside Design Plus
Cover design by Jon McGrath
Cover Photo: Veer

First printing 2008

Printed in the United States of America

Trade Paperback ISBN: 978-1-58134-887-3
PDF ISBN: 978-1-4335-0427-3
MobiPocket ISBN: 978-1-4335-0428-0

Library of Congress Cataloging-in-Publication Data

Carter, Anthony J., 1967–
    Experiencing the truth : bringing the Reformation to the African-American church / Anthony J. Carter, Kenneth Jones, and Michael Leach / edited by Anthony J. Carter.
        p. cm.
    Includes bibliographical references and index.
    ISBN 978-1-58134-887-3 (tpb)
    1. Reformed Church—Doctrines. 2. African Americans—Religion. I. Jones, Kenneth, 1946– II. Leach, Michael, 1940– III. Carter, Anthony J., 1967– IV. Title.

BX9422.3.C37 2008
284′.208996073—dc22   2008008278

VP		16	15	14	13	12	11	10	09	08
		9	8	7	6	5	4	3	2	1

CONTENTS

1. Experiencing the Truth: An Introduction   7
   Anthony J. Carter

2. Biblical Theology: Experiencing the Truth about God   23
   Michael Leach

3. Biblical Preaching: Experiencing the Word of God   55
   Anthony J. Carter

4. Biblical Worship: Experiencing the Presence of God   79
   Anthony J. Carter

5. Biblical Spirituality: Experiencing the Spirit of God   107
   Kenneth Jones

6. Grace So Amazing: Experiencing the Doctrines of
      Grace   141
   Anthony J. Carter

   Appendix 1: Sermon Preparation   155
   Appendix 2: Sample Sermon Outline   159
   Appendix 3: Sample Orders of Worship   167

   Notes   173
   Index   183

1

EXPERIENCING THE TRUTH
An Introduction

by ANTHONY J. CARTER

Are you attending the wrong church? This question was the topic of an article in *Gospel Today Magazine.*[1] According to the article, much has been written addressing the absence of men in most churches today. Yet, little attention has been paid to the men who are in church and the reasons why they attend the church they do. There is a nonchalant, almost disinterested quality to the men who are in church. The reason, according to the journalist, is that many of these men are in churches not of their own choosing. Consequently, they may be in the wrong place for the wrong reason. What are these reasons? Topping the journalist's list:

1. It was the church of your childhood or the church where you first received Christ.
2. It's where you found the love of your life.
3. It's conveniently located.
4. The music is good.
5. The pastor is cool.
6. It was recommended by a friend.[2]

Contrary to what many might think, these are not sufficient grounds for attending a church. The selection of a church home is an important and life-impacting decision. Therefore it should be done soberly, intentionally, and with prayer and counsel. Apparently, the author of the aforementioned article agrees. He offers six answers to the question, what should a man look for when selecting a church?

1. Look for a church where other men are actively involved in the ministry, and not just the men's ministry.
2. Look for a church where you can find purpose and significance for your life.
3. Look for a church where manhood is celebrated and not desecrated.
4. Look for a church where there is a connection between the pulpit and the pew.
5. Look for a church where opportunities for leadership exist.
6. Look for a church where the needs of the rest of your family are met.[3]

Honestly, a man could just as well find the above listing fulfilled in a national fraternity or a local golf club. In reading the journalist's suggestions, one is struck by the accuracy with which he unknowingly demonstrates the malady and even calamity that is the church in general and the predominantly African-American church in particular. In setting forth his suggestions for determining one's church home, the author prioritizes issues of felt needs and a self-serving agenda. He fails to demonstrate the biblical knowledge and discernment that is needed to inform such an important decision, yet rarely does.

Sadly, there is no mention of the single most important aspect of any decision to attend a church. The first and fundamental question should be: Is the Word of God faithfully and clearly expounded? Closely related to the first question are subsequent important questions: Are the sacraments faithfully administered? Is God the focus of the worship in word and song? Are faithfulness and holiness in life promoted? Ultimately: Are the theology of the pulpit and the practice of pew consistent with biblical, historic, experiential Christianity? These are the questions every Christian should be asking. These are the questions rarely raised in the predominantly African-American church today. These are the questions that precipitate the writing of this book.

The dearth of biblical truth among Christians today is caused by their search for places that serve them and meet their perceived needs rather than places where God is exalted and Christ is trusted because the Word of God is faithfully proclaimed. Yet, it is not only because people are looking for churches that will focus on their perceived felt needs; churches who are advertising themselves as places where people can get whatever they want, when they want it, and how they want it are equally responsible. This has created a chasm between Christianity in predominantly African-American churches and true, biblical Christian experience. Into this chasm we seek to posit historic, Reformed theology.

In *On Being Black and Reformed*, I argued for the legitimate correlation of the African-American Christian experience and historic, Reformed theology.[4] While some have thought that these two perspectives are antithetical, I suggested that they are inherently complementary, and when brought together they reveal a beautiful symphony of truth and experience that God desires for his people to know. In fact, Reformed, biblical theology should serve as the foundation of all experiential truth, particularly the experience of African-Americans.

To see the African-American Christian experience apart from an intentional application of Reformed theological principles is like reading a book by the moonlight. We can see the page well enough to make out the story, but it is so much easier and indeed enlightening to read by the direct light of the noonday sun. Reformed theology shines the noonday sun upon Christian experience so that we see more and further than we could by moonlight. By understanding Reformed theology, the history of African-Americans (and any other people for that matter) is enriched because the biblical God as understood in Reformed theology is big and gracious. He is sovereign and sophisticated. He is to be celebrated and feared.

In this present work, I have enlisted the help of some friends in bringing the truth of Reformed theology not simply to African-American history and experience, but also in bringing it to the church today—the whole of Christianity in general and the predominantly African-American church in particular. It is our hope that you will see that biblical, Reformed theology is not only essential in accurately discerning what God has done, but it is imperative if we are to understand what God is doing and what he is calling his people to be in our time. Though the times may seem bleak, we are convinced of the illuminating power of the gospel of truth.

It was Dr. Martin Luther King Jr. who reminded us that only when it is dark enough can one see the stars. The state of the church in general and the African-American church in particular is dark. The darkness is not due to a lack of attendance on Sunday mornings at places that call themselves churches. It is not due to a lack of interest in spiritual things. No. Black men and women go to church. Black men and women want to know about God. George Barna, in his research for *High Impact African-American Churches*, posed the following questions after analyzing his data:

> Do you know that we tested 22 common goals that people pursue, the top rated goal among black adults is to have a close relationship with God, while the same goal is ranked fifth by whites? Or that being actively involved in a church is a goal pursued by three-quarters of all black adults but by less than half of all white adults?[5]

The growth of the mega-church among African-Americans in recent years is staggering. There is no lack of buildings opened in the name of God. Our neighborhoods are littered with places of worship, with more being built and bought every day. Again, Barna makes the point when his research reveals that:

> There is a higher percentage of large black congregations than there is among white or Hispanic congregations. In fact, while Willow Creek and Saddleback are regularly touted by the media as the biggest

churches in North America, there are at least a dozen black churches whose attendance exceeds either of those well known congregations by at least a couple thousand people per week![6]

No, the problem and the darkness in predominantly African-American churches are not from a lack of construction or the absence of congregants, but rather a lack of content. The problem lies in the character and quality of the Christianity that these places promote and export.

Open-Bible Reformation

In a much talked about article in the *Washington Post*, journalist John Fountain lamented the present state of the predominantly African-American church. In Fountain's own testimony, he has lost confidence in the church. He has become disillusioned with the direction the predominantly African-American church has taken. He has found the drive for wealth and success that is popularized by the mega-church movement to be distasteful and offensive. According to Fountain:

> I am angered by the preacher I know, and his wife and co-pastor, who exacted a per diem and drove luxury vehicles, their modest salaries boosted by tithes and offerings from poor folks in a struggling congregation of families, a number of them headed by single women. This at a time when the church didn't own a single chair and was renting a building to hold worship services.[7]

Yet every Sunday large churches and small ones are filled with men and women seeking to drive luxury vehicles and boost their financial worth because the preacher told them that Jesus was rich and they should be rich too. Too many of these places are filled with men and women who know too little of the truth contained in Scripture and too little of the truth about the God of Scripture, because they spend too much of their time ingesting the error dispensed by preachers and teachers who fancy themselves apostles, prophets, bishops, and pastors.

In the growing black mega-church movement, there is an overwhelming emphasis upon the sensational, excitable, and experiential. There is an unbiblical infatuation with the miraculous and the fanciful. This produces a vacuum where objective biblical truth is sucked up and finds little place in the life of the church or the Christian. Again, Fountain's disillusionment is due in large part to this experience-driven type of Christianity, which he experienced. According to Fountain:

> I am the grandson of a pastor and am myself a licensed minister. I love God and I love the church. I know church-speak and feel as comfortable shouting hallelujahs and amens and lifting my hands in the sanctuary as I do putting on my socks. I have danced in the spirit, spoken in tongues, and proclaimed Jesus Christ as my Lord and savior. I once arrived faithfully at the door of every prayer meeting and went to nearly every Bible study and month-long revival. I attended umpteen services, even the midnight musicals and my church's annual national meetings, like the one held two weeks ago in Kansas City. Yet I now feel disconnected. I *am* disconnected. Not necessarily from God, but from the church.[8]

Unfortunately for Fountain and many with similar testimonies, church has become nothing but a heavy dose of emotional stimulation. And when the emotional high has worn off, he begins looking for meetings to attend to find that energy. He begins looking for work to do to make him once again feel significant. Here is a glaring and sad illustration of a man who thinks he experienced God, when perhaps all he experienced was religious experience itself.

So, what is needed in this malaise of Christianity that is commonly experienced on Sunday mornings? What should our answer be to this celebrity-driven, glitter and glory brand of Christianity? What is the answer to John Fountain and many more who find popular Christianity in the predominantly black church shallow and uninspired? Fountain could use a Christianity that does not simply accentuate the novel and promote the excitable, but seeks to articulate and demonstrate a faith grounded in historical theology and proclaimed with contemporary relevance. Such Christianity is not popular in our day, yet it is most needed. Such has been the Christianity articulated in the historic Reformed tradition.

In speaking at a pastor conference in Miami in 2005, Ken Jones said that a reformation is needed, but not like those reformations in the past.[9] In Josiah's day (2 Kings 23) the people needed a reformation because the Word of God was lost. Josiah led the people of God in finding and restoring the Word in their midst. The Second Reformation was under Martin Luther (1483–1546). This Reformation was not needed because the Word of God was lost, but because the Word of God was closed. Luther led the people of God in the rediscovery of the truth by opening the Bible to all people. In our day, the Word of God is not lost nor is it closed. We have open Bibles every Sunday all over the country. We need a reformation today because the Word of God is misinterpreted and misappropriated. In other words, we need an open-Bible Reformation!

Why Reformed Theology?

Why is it necessary that Reformed theology be posited as the answer to much of what plagues the church, particularly the predominantly African-American expression of the church? Two reasons come to mind.

A Biblically-Grounded Faith

Christianity in America, and particularly the predominantly African-American expression of Christianity, has sought to be a biblical faith, and Reformed theology has presented the most biblically consistent expression of Christianity and Christian thought known to the world.

I know, some will find that statement a bit exaggerated and may want to charge it to unfettered enthusiasm. Yet I don't state it out of sheer enthusiasm (though I am enthusiastic). Rather I say it with the settled conviction that it is a matter of substantiated fact. You see, no other expression of Protestant Christianity has been as careful to make sure its understanding and expression of theology has been consistently biblical than has the Reformed tradition.

No one would argue that rigorous theological study and proclamation has been a distinctive of Reformed Christianity. And thus the Reformed tradition has served the church best in this regard. The Reformed tradition has produced the great confessions and catechisms of the Faith. From *Luther's Catechisms* to the *Heidelberg Catechism*; from the *Canons of Dordt* to the *Belgic Confession*; from the *Westminster Confession and Catechisms* to the *Thirty-nine Articles* to the *1689 Baptist Confession* and *Philadelphia Confession*; even to the more contemporary documents of the *Cambridge Declaration* and the *Chicago Statement on Biblical Inerrancy* and the recent affirmations and denials of the *Together for the Gospel Statement*—Reformed theology has led the way in making sure that the theology articulated by the church is biblical theology. It has sought to guard the parameters of said theology with biblical confessions and to pass along to the next generation those theological commitments through the catechisms. Each of these confessions and catechisms is filled with references to Scripture and seeks to articulate the faith with the Bible—and the Bible alone—serving as the authority and foundation.

The great theological works in the history of the Protestant church and the men who produced them further demonstrate the influence of the Reformed tradition. Make a short list of the most influential and substantial theological works in the history of the church and you will find it dominated by Reformed preachers and theologians. Consider the works of Martin Luther (*Bondage of the Will*) and John Calvin (*Institutes of the Christian Religion*). It could be said of Calvin's seminal work that all theology subsequent to Calvin has in one way or another been a response to or a furthering of Calvin. How about John Owen, Jonathan Edwards, Thomas Watson, and John Bunyan? Bunyan's *Pilgrim's Progress* is arguably the most recognizable and read piece of literature in the world next to the Bible. Read Bunyan's masterful work and you will see nothing but the richest, most experiential and pastoral Reformed theology you'll find anywhere. The list would also include preachers like Charles Spurgeon and D. Martyn Lloyd-Jones and theologians like B. B. Warfield, Louis Berkhof, J. I. Packer, and R. C. Sproul. The list could go on and on; the impact that the writings of Reformed preachers and theologians have made upon the world is incalculable.

No one could honestly argue against this. What other Protestant tradition can set forth confessions and statements of faith even remotely comparable to those of the Reformed tradition? And why is this the case? Why has the Reformed tradition been so rigorous in its theological commitments? It begins with the Reformed commitment to the inspiration and authority of Scripture.

Reformed theology has led the way since the time of the Reformation in defending and promoting the veracity of the Scriptures. It is committed to the Reformation's slogan, s*ola Scriptura* (or "Scripture alone"), which means that the Bible alone is the final and only infallible authority for faith, life, and conduct in the church and the Christian life.

In the often recurring battle for the Bible, Reformation-minded Christians have always been on the front lines. Even those who are not particularly sympathetic to Reformed theology would have to admit that the Protestant church owes a debt of gratitude to Calvinists and the Reformed thinkers for their ready and consistent defense of the Bible's inspiration and authority. From the Reformation's call to put a Bible in the hands of the people, to B. B. Warfield's *Inspiration and Authority of the Bible*, to the *Chicago Statement on Biblical Inerrancy*, the history of Reformed theology has been one of defending the inspiration and inerrancy of the Scriptures.

Consequently, for the Reformed Christian the Bible serves as the foundation of truth and submission to the Scriptures; as the Word of God, it guides all of life, particularly preaching and worship. In Reformed thought God is sovereign; he is in control of and the Lord over all creation. Nothing in all of creation moves or breathes or acts outside of his providential hand. Why? Not because some theologians got together in a dark, smoke-filled room and decided to think of ways to express God so he would seem to be all-powerful and all-knowing even though he's not. It is because the Bible says it's true:

[The Lord's] dominion is an everlasting dominion,
>   and his kingdom endures from generation to generation;
all the inhabitants of the earth are accounted as nothing,
>   and he does according to his will among the host of heaven
>   and among the inhabitants of the earth;
and none can stay his hand
>   or say to him, "What have you done?" (Dan. 4:34–35).

The second reason why Reformed theology is the answer is like the first.

An Experiential Faith

Christianity is an experiential faith. That is to say that the God the Bible proclaims is a God who can not only be known, but can and should be experienced. Reformed theology, when rightly understood and proclaimed, is the most truly experiential form of Christianity.

This might sound strange and even laughable to opponents of Reformed Christianity, because one of the most common and frequently expressed charges against Reformed theology is that it is an emotionless, life-killing, and passionless expression of Christianity. This characterization has led to the commonly used expression "the frozen chosen."

Admittedly, the reason why this characterization is so prevalent is because at times those who have advocated Reformed theology have been men and women who have emphasized its theological rigor and intellectualism, but not its life and passion.

D. Martyn Lloyd-Jones, the late Reformed theologian and pastor of Westminster Chapel in London, once said that the Calvinist always lives with the threat of being too theoretical. This was due, according to Lloyd-Jones, to the fact that the more intelligent a man or woman was, the more likely he or she was to be a Calvinist, because Calvinism demands thought and study. You've got to read books and consider doctrine. And so there is always the danger, according to Lloyd-Jones, of becoming an intellectualist.[10]

Unfortunately, honesty compels us to admit that this charge too often has proven true. Too often Reformed theology produces adherents who are dry and cold in their affections. Too often it has been preached from pulpits that were dry and cold. In fact, one of the reasons why Presbyterians and the Reformed do not have a long and fruitful history among African-Americans is because of this dry intellectualism. According to the testimony of Richard Allen, founder of the African Methodist Episcopal Church:

> The Methodist were the first people that brought glad tidings to colored people . . . for all the other denominations preached so high flown that we were not able to comprehend their doctrine.[11]

What do we say to such charges? First we admit that from time to time we have been cold. And among some Reformed churches and Christians this is still true. Yet we also assert that this is not necessary to a true expression of Reformed theology. Historically Reformed theology has been highly experiential, emotionally stimulating, and passionately preached. True Reformed preaching is not simply a scholastic pursuit. The Reformed preacher, according to Wilhelmus à Brakel, will make "his astute theological acumen subservient to the glory of God and the spiritual welfare of His church." He makes this point when he instructs ministers:

> He [the minister] ought to use all his scholarship to formulate the matters to be presented, in order that he might express them in the clearest and most powerful manner. While using his scholarship, however, he must conceal his scholarship in the pulpit.[12]

Wilhelmus à Brakel is one of my favorite theologians. Most people today are not familiar with him, but during the Second Reformation of the seventeenth century, à Brakel was among the most respected and most read Dutch Reformed pastors and theologians. He wrote my favorite treatise on systematic theology titled *The Christian's Reasonable Service*. I believe it sets forth Reformed theology in its most biblical, historical, and most importantly, experiential form. One à Brakel biographer writes:

The uniqueness of àBrakel's work lies in the fact that it is more than a systematic theology . . . àBrakel's intent in writing is inescapable: He intensely wishes that the truth expounded may become an experiential reality in the hearts of those who read. In a masterful way he establishes the crucial relationship between objective truth and the subjective experience of that truth.[13]

Experiencing the truth—that is what Reformed theology is all about! True Christian experience is not experience for experience's sake. That type of Christianity is the error too often found in Pentecostalism and neo-Pentecostalism, where the experience with the truth (namely the Spirit of Truth) supposedly only occurs when some excitable, emotional, and even spasmodic outburst has been seen or heard. And yet, often this is nothing more than an experience with experience, which is satisfactory for a moment but ultimately produces no lasting fruit and leaves its adherent in a worse spiritual and intellectual state. Indeed, this was the case with John Fountain.

Unfortunately for Fountain and many with similar testimonies, church has become nothing but a heavy dose of emotional stimulation. What is the answer for Fountain and others like him? What is the hope for a Christianity today that is nothing more than men and women chasing one emotional high after the other?

The answer to this subjective, irrational approach to the Christian faith, interestingly, is not the dry, rational intellectualism that is popularly portrayed in Reformed American thought. Rather, it is the experiential Christianity that is objectively based but subjectively experienced. Biblical Christianity is always establishing the relationship between objective truth and subjective experience. And as a projection of biblical Christianity, true Reformed theology is always seeking to do the same. According to à Brakel, the end of true Reformed theology is an experience with the Spirit of Truth to the end of:

the conversion of the unconverted, the instruction of the ignorant, the restoration of the backsliders, the encouragement of the discouraged, as well as to the growth of faith, hope, and love in all who have become partakers of a measure of grace.[14]

The best Reformed biblical theology is not found in ivory towers or monastic huddles, but in the everyday experiences of life in a fallen world being redeemed by God. Understanding this, we say, without apology, that Reformed theology is the hope of Christianity. It has been the hope of Christianity since the Reformation, and it continues to be the hope today.

Calling the African-American Church Back

By positing Reformed theology as the truth worth experiencing in the predominantly black church, we are not attempting to re-invent the theological wheel. Instead we want to call the church back to the faith that has been articulated in the Scriptures and has long been advanced by the church (much of this truth has been ascribed in the church's historic creeds and confessions). The Reformation was successful not because it was new or promoted new revelatory knowledge. On the contrary, it was successful because in bringing back the glorious gospel of grace it sought God's glory through the recovery of his Word.

Michael Leach and Kenneth Jones have joined me in an effort to re-present Reformed theology to the predominantly African-American church.

Biblical Theology (by Michael Leach). Mike begins the body of this book by laying the theological foundations for our proposal. He defines what biblical, experiential theology is. He then systematically and biblically sets forth the case for Reformed biblical theology and demonstrates how this theology is inherently experiential and best articulates the biblical view of what the church is and what it should be.

Biblical Preaching (by Anthony Carter). I define what biblical preaching is and how important it is to the church. I make the case for preaching that is Reformed, historical, and experiential. I also express the correlation between historic black preaching and Reformed theology and how the two naturally complement each other. In addition, appendixes 1 and 2 include some practical steps in sermon preparation, as well as a sample sermon.

Biblical Worship (by Anthony Carter). I address the subject of worship—its form and content in the church today. I define what biblical worship is and what it is not. I provide the case for Reformed, experiential, biblical worship within the predominantly African-American church and issue a plea to see the Word of God as central to all we do in worship. I also offer samples of orders of worship from predominantly black churches that hold to Reformed theology in appendix 2.

Biblical Spirituality (by Kenneth Jones). Ken Jones answers, How now should we live? In other words, Ken speaks of biblical sanctification. He looks at the development of African-American spirituality, its downturn, and the need for a biblical recovery. For this recovery, Jones sets forth true, biblical, Reformed, experiential spirituality that is based in a trust in the sufficiency of the inerrant Word of God.

A Reformation for This Generation

Our goal in this book is to add fuel to the fire that is this generation's glorious reformation. And this one must be summed up in the two Latin phrases that found prominence during the sixteenth-century Reformation: *Post tenebras lux* and *non nobis Domine*.

Post tenebras lux is translated "after darkness, light." This slogan identified the essence of the Reformation. Luther and the other reformers were not attempting to reinvent the church, only to shed light upon the darkness of its doctrine and worship. It was their belief that truth would win out over error, if truth would be known. Today we have the same conviction. The church does not need to be reinvented, God forbid. It once again needs the light of the truth that is the glorious and biblical doctrines recovered during the Reformation. The darkness that has enveloped the church will by God's grace and in his providence give way to a light—brilliant and wonderful. It is a light that is beginning to shine through this present darkness. What a great light it will be! As the prophet said, "The people who walked in darkness have seen a great light; those who dwelt in a land of deep darkness, on them has light shined" (Isa. 9:2).

Non nobis Domine, translated "not to us, Lord," is taken from the first line of Psalm 115. The Reformers understood that if God were going to restore his glory and majesty to the church once again, it was going to be for his name and for his glory alone. And if God would visit his people, he would do so for his name and his glory alone. They knew that the glory of God was in the Gospel of Christ. Subsequently, they all with a singular voice wrote and preached, "Not to us, O LORD, not to us, but to your name give glory" (Ps. 115:1). Today will be no different. The reformation that we pray and labor for in the church in general (and the African-American church in particular) is a reformation that will only come because God determines to glorify himself through us and to us, not for our glory, but for his alone. So we, like the magisterial reformers, proclaim and pray *non nobis Domine*. It is my prayer that it will be the undercurrent and foundation of all we write, preach, and pray.

Today, we find ourselves in a dark place, yet the light of the truth of the Scriptures continues to shine brightly. All over this country, and indeed around the world, men and women, particularly those of African descent, are falling out of love with the world and the worldliness of popular television-driven Christianity, and falling in love with the biblical, historic faith that was and is found in Reformed theology. As we write this book, we are full of optimism and hope. We are witnessing the rise of a new generation of African-American Christians who see through the fading glory of the empty way of life advocated by the false prosperity gospel, and are seeing more clearly the faith that has once and for all been delivered to the saints—the faith rediscovered during the Reformation and being reenergized in our time. This book is part of our ongoing dedication to this move of God. We believe that God is always reforming his people according to his Spirit by his Word.

It is our sincerest desire to see God move by his Spirit to revive the church in our day according to the old paths of heart-felt and head-intoxicated experiential Christianity. To this end we have written this book, and to this end we do pray that all those who read the thoughts contained here will be moved to preach, promote, and practice a historic, biblical, and experiential Christianity to the glory of God in Christ Jesus and the good of his people called by his name.

Soli Deo Gloria!

2

BIBLICAL THEOLOGY
Experiencing the Truth about God

by MICHAEL LEACH

What do you mean, you sleeper? Arise, call out to your god!
Perhaps the god will give a thought to us, that we may not perish
(Jonah 1:6).

Worldliness is the bane of the church and the robber of her
theology. It could be argued that the modern church is like Jonah.
It is comfortable in its carnality and is soundly sleeping at the bottom of the boat. So great is the impact of the world on it, that it has
divested itself of its distinctive message, language, and sound. I fear
that in many respects, today's church is so dependent on secular
culture that it is constantly borrowing from it in order to be more
easily understood in its claims, more relevant in its message, and
more user-friendly in its praxis.

Some have rightly said that the church and the world have "much
in the showroom and nothing in the stockroom." That is to say, the

premier characteristic of our modern churches is their overwhelming superficiality. Instead of being renowned for their theological soundness, doctrinal purity, evangelical authenticity, and biblical fidelity, the church seems to have more in common with secular places of entertainment than with its historical, biblical definition as the people of the holy, transcendent, eternal God. In this regard, we painfully recall the trenchant sarcasm of former Tennessee senator and television and movie screen actor, Fred Thompson, when he quipped before the Commonwealth Club of California, "After two years in Washington, I often long for the realism and sincerity of Hollywood."[1]

We are weeping today because the pervasive flippancy and levity of our times have so overrun the church that the irresistible thrust to be entertaining rules over it with an unassailable sovereignty. The seething desire to be relevant, practical, relational, up-to-date, and helpful is transforming the church into a seeker-pleasing, seeker-gathering institution, increasingly molded by the world while at the same time it sheepishly claims to be the citadel of Christ. This growing syncretism is producing such a bothersome blend that one justly fears that the term *church*, much like the word *Christian*, is undergoing such a momentous deconstruction as to render it unidentifiable from its biblical foundations.

After Light, Darkness

Popular religion, as flaunted on television and proclaimed in the vast majority of the large so-called evangelical churches testifies to the daunting reality that we are now re-entering a neo-medieval period of darkness. A fitting slogan for today's religious community may well be *post lucem, tenebrae*: after light, darkness.[2]

The current darkness has a unique characteristic. It is not one which, like a fog or a billow of smoke, slowly advances from one corner of a city to the other, menacingly making its way until the entire area lies under its darkening haze. Rather, it is more like a pandemic shadow that is already hovering over the land and that is increasing in density as well as penetration. It is a grim spectacle indeed, for there are few oases of refreshing sunlight.

The Black Church Is Impacted

The black church is not exempt from this sweeping malaise. As part of the national religious landscape, it is also guilty of the vicious illness enveloping U.S. evangelicalism. Like the church at large, it also suffers from a blatant rejection of the Scriptures alone as the final and only absolute standard of truth in all matters of faith and conduct; a distorted view of preaching that now promises temporal prosperity, personal therapy, and individual glory; a shocking loss of the eternal and transcendent as its governing priorities; a distressing de-emphasis of the nature and significance of the sacraments; a vacuous understanding of the meaning and practice of kingdom discipleship; a human-centered, consumeristic notion of worship; and a truncated view of the church, ministry, and missions.

Given this dim background, as well as the significance of this work, this chapter attempts to set a biblical-theological paradigm for the remaining sections. Therefore we must engage with the prevailing notions of theology in the church as a whole and in the African-American church in particular.

The Need for Sound Theology

The truth this present work seeks to unveil is the overwhelming need for the understanding and application of sound biblical theology in all areas of faith and life. There is a thick and dominant strand within the pale of black religion that holds that blacks are not interested in the historic doctrines of the faith. Supposedly, blacks are mainly preoccupied with the application of Scripture to their pressing existential conditions. As a result, many African-Americans tend to neglect in-depth studies of the rich doctrines of the Christian faith such as the Trinity, the deity and humanity of Christ, the consubstantiality of the Son with the Father, the substitutionary atonement of Christ, the components of faith, the order of salvation (that is to say, the orderly process by which the Holy Spirit applies the benefits of Christ's redemptive work to the hearts of God's chosen people), and many others. Foundational terms such as redemption, regeneration, justification, reconciliation, covenant, sanctification, and glorification have fallen into the categories of a foreign language and would sound alien in many of our churches. Strangely, the reason for this neglect is not primarily that of disagreement, or of theological abstruseness, or even of some perceived logical incoherence, but rather because these subjects are considered to be non-essential in answering the existential question, how shall we then live? In other words, it is believed that for blacks the heavy emphasis on the application of Scripture precludes the need for a well-rounded theological foundation. In such thinking, the need for a systematic probing into the profound mysteries and truths of Christianity is replaced by an overemphasis upon applying Scripture to contemporary existential settings.

Doctrine versus Duty

A study of the supposedly most effective black churches in the United States showed that while these churches acknowledged the overwhelming need to apply the timeless, universal truths of Scripture in the context of everyday life, so as "to make theology relevant to the common man and to the common condition," their emphasis on this necessary application betrayed a deep-seated antipathy toward the historic Christian doctrines. In the words of one author:

> We simply do not identify . . . with many of the *complex, esoteric, and impersonal theological concepts or doctrines* held up before us. Indeed, while theologians go to extraordinary lengths to re-conceptualize and articulate the life of faith, the actual struggle to find theology practical wrestles with the meaning of life and the daily experiences of living.[3]

In other words, in their haste to apply biblical teaching to local and temporal conditions, the most effective black churches actually exhibit an ingrained tendency to belittle the historic doctrines of the faith "once delivered to all the saints."[4]

Obviously, such a situation bristles with several problems, one of which is the fallacy of the false dilemma or the either/or fallacy. In the words of one observer:

> [T]heology, if it is true, is lived. It is lived in the life of the church, those whom God has called out from a rebellious world. Moreover, it is lived in the midst of the world, not in isolation from it. God has not removed the church from the world of rebellion, nor has he removed the world of rebellion from within the church.[5]

To say the least, theology is intrinsically practical. Its very content, the character and work of the infinite, sovereign, and holy God in history, inescapably requires the fitting response of all his creatures.

The ensuing disaster of such a false division is manifest. In spite of the dizzying religious activities in most predominantly black churches—activity marked by Bible reading, Sunday school and worship attendance, prayer, and fasting—far outstripping that of whites and Hispanics, a recent poll revealed that:

- 22 percent of the black respondents deny the existence of Satan.
- Only 27 percent affirm the reality of absolute moral truth.
- Fewer than 50 percent uphold the need to witness to Christ and his work in their lives.
- 30 percent agree that good works can merit salvation.
- A staggering 52 percent deny the sinlessness of Jesus Christ.[6]

The last two points are most crucial: a significant percentage of the respondents believe in a salvation by works scheme while a majority deny the perfect character of Jesus Christ, in spite of the clear and contrary teaching of such biblical texts as 2 Corinthians 5:21 and Hebrews 4:15; 7:26.

The matter becomes even clearer when George Barna and Harry Jackson state that blacks' faith in Jesus Christ is their ultimate safety net, "a powerful means of understanding the tragedies and disappointments of life *even if their theology is not fully defensible on biblical grounds.*[7] Here, a few observations are necessary.

First, apart from being manifestly erroneous and unbiblical, the above findings highlight the grave danger we face when we elevate our experiences above the need to be solidly planted on the unmovable foundation of biblical truth. What we really have is the claim of a genuine Christian experience that is based upon unbiblical grounds. This amounts to defining Christianity in unbiblical terms. The result is a patent illustration of not only the rejection of biblical truth but also of the pervasive peril of postmodern, irrational thought. Scripture never posits a separation between doctrine and duty, beliefs and behavior. On the contrary, the biblical witness to the relationship of belief and practice is one that must emphasize the inseparability of this tandem in such a way that the former is the foundation for the latter and in turn strengthens and confirms it.

Second, such a view misses the fact that the very "complex, esoteric, and impersonal" theological points serve to clarify the God we are to worship. Without a clear and accurate knowledge of him as he reveals himself on the pages of Scripture, we incur the tragic risks of worshiping another god, preaching another gospel, and, consequently, living another life (other than the Christian life).[8]

Many of the cardinal doctrines of Christianity were crystallized in the heated furnace of intense theological debate against heretical positions that were striving for ascendancy. In his superintending providence, God has protected and preserved them in the struggles and has caused them to be embodied in such historic documents as the Apostles' Creed, the Nicene Creed, the Athanasian Creed, the Canons of Dordt, and many others. Our knowledge of this history should therefore be characterized by more than a scant familiarity with these documents and doctrines; it should foster within us at least two fitting responses: a profound appreciation for our faithful forebears, many of whom defended these doctrines at the cost of their lives, and also a holy gratitude to our God for opening our eyes to understand them.

Unfortunately, evangelicalism has chosen to embrace an antihistorical perspective and to demean the importance of these creeds and confessions. It is a general but safe assessment that regardless of ethnic composition, our churches are now decidedly experiential rather than confessional. A sound knowledge of all that we can possibly know about the nature of our God and his works in creation and redemption can serve only to strengthen our love for him, enrich our worship of him, and intensify our witness and work for him.

Third, the belittling of sound theology necessarily results in pragmatic expediency:

> When churches abandon or de-emphasize theology, they give up the intellectual tools by which the Christian message can be articulated and defended. In the resulting chaos of religious ideas, the principal criterion left to the community as it seeks to find its way is quite naturally, that of expediency.[9]

Richard Lints's admonition is apropos. The stifling or diminishing of theology leads to an impoverished idea of God and quickly deteriorates into a system that is embraced not because it is God-glorifying and God-enjoying, but because it produces desired results. Rather than asking the controlling questions, who is this redeeming God that sent his eternal Son to die for sinners? and what does he require of us? we instead ponder, what do I need to do so that he can relieve me of my family, financial, or professional problems? In this scenario, the enduring wonder of an ineffable God is ruthlessly replaced by the expedient measures constrained by our desire to improve our temporal circumstances.

A Reformed Emphasis

In light of the present condition, our conviction and solution is to once again emphasize the lofty distinctives of the Reformed tradition, incorporate the doctrines that have been handed down to us from the collective wisdom of the historical church, and strive to return to the biblical gospel rather than "plunge ourselves back to the biases of our own individual situations."[10]

To begin with, the issue before us is not how sincerely or passionately we think about God but whether our thoughts reflect the Person and works of the Triune God as he declares himself in his two books—that of nature (general revelation) and that of the Bible (special revelation). The questions before us have to do with whether our views of God accurately and consistently portray him in the absolute perfection and manifold excellencies of his attributes as he reveals them to us in Scripture. Is our understanding of God derived from Scripture alone, or is it mainly the product of human tradition? Is it a sinister amalgam of his self-disclosure in Scripture along with the opinions and speculations of folklore? What has he done and what is he doing in his creation? How can we be sure that our view of God is correct?

With these basic challenges in mind, let us first study *theology*.

What Is Theology?

Theology may be defined as "the *science concerning God* that is established upon His voluntary self-revelation to man."[11] Using this definition, we see that there is an external, objective character of God's self-revelation to his creatures. Subsequently, maintaining the objective dimension of theology is not a matter of choice but of pressing necessity, a necessity that is determined by two conditions: the Creator/creature distinction and the intrusion of sin. These two facts compel us to acknowledge the divine initiative, a pervasive aspect of God's interaction with his creation, in all areas of creation and redemption.[12]

The Creator/Creature Distinction
The *Westminster Confession of Faith* comments on the Creator/creature distinction as follows:

> The distance between God and the creature is so great, that although reasonable creatures do owe obedience unto him as their Creator, yet they could never have any fruition of him as their blessedness and reward, but by some voluntary condescension on God's part, which he hath been pleased to express by way of covenant.[13]

Here the *Confession* admits of an unbridgeable chasm between God the Creator and man the creature. The biblical record is clear that man, even in the purity of his pre-fallen condition, could not approach God for the sake of establishing a relationship with him. Even when Adam had no need of a mediator between himself and his Creator (a mediator is only necessary when estranged parties need to be reconciled), there was no ontological equality between God and man.[14] That is to say, God and man are not the same in essence and never will be, neither in the pristine conditions of a world untainted by sin nor in the perfect, eternal bliss of heaven where the redeemed of God will dwell with him face to face. God will always be God and man will always be creature, and at no time shall the twain meet. "Between God as the Creator and all other things as created the distinction is absolute. There is not such another gulf within the universe."[15]

The inseparable disparity between Creator and creature is also identified by man's obligation to obey his Creator. Notice the normative duty of this relationship—man is required to grant full obedience to his Creator simply because man is his creature; in other words, here we learn the timeless principle that *by nature creaturehood means servanthood.* Therefore, it is in the creature's highest interest to render unfeigned obedience to his Maker. Since the relationship between Creator and creature does not change, we can safely conclude that such obligation continues throughout eternity.

The *Confession* strongly implies that the consequence of this faithful obedience of creature to Creator is the creature's experiencing God as "his blessedness and reward." The emphasis is that God himself, not the righteous works he performs on our behalf or the manifold gifts and graces he freely offers us, is our ultimate blessing and goodness. That is to say, our Creator has made us and designed us to exist in an eternal relationship with him, promising us fullness of life upon our perfect, personal, and permanent obedience to him.[16] The distinction between Creator and creature also points to an eternal dependence of man on God.

The Divine Initiative in Creation and Redemption

God does not leave man in his condition of irreducible, eternal distance from God. Rather, according to his general, indiscriminate compassion and love for his creature, God voluntarily condescends or lowers himself to man's level and unilaterally establishes a covenant of works with him to facilitate Adam's reception of the supreme privileges and glorious benefits that are to be found in his Creator.

Of paramount importance is the fact that God himself initiates this relationship. This divine condescension is essentially the self-revelation of God to his creatures. "God must come to us before we can go to him"; he must open up "the mystery of his nature" before the creature can gain any knowledge of him.[17] That is to say, since God precedes all creation—he is infinite and eternal—and is known to himself alone, his eternal pre-existence necessarily means that he has first to call into being a creature before any extraneous knowledge of God is available or even possible. *"Creation therefore was the first step in the production of extra-divine knowledge"*[18]

How different is this process in all other sciences in which man stands alongside the objects of his investigation, assumes the initiative in studying his objects, subjects them to his scrutiny, and then compels them to submit to his study! In theology the reverse is true. It is God who is always proactive in revealing his nature to man whom he has created in his image, that man may receive the knowledge of the divine, infinite perfections with his finite mind. For these reasons, we are obliged to conclude that "God as distinct from the creature, is the only legitimate object of Theology."[19]

This divine priority in creation and redemption, manifest in God's Word and deed, is a refreshing cord coursing its way throughout Scripture. For example, the radical and polemical words, "In the beginning God created the heavens and the earth" signal the divine initiative in bringing everything outside of himself into being by successive processes of divine fiat. Likewise in redemption, Scripture tells us that in eternity past, before he had even created the world, the Father had already chosen, predestined, adopted, and given a special number of sinners to the Son, for the Father's own glory (John 6:37; 17:6; Eph. 1:3–14; see John 6:44; 1 Pet. 1:3). This divine priority continues in our sanctification as Scripture also teaches us that we are to walk according to the Spirit and to be led by him (Rom. 8:1, 14; Gal. 5:18) and to live by him (Gal. 5:25). While our sanctification or growth into Christ requires us to "work out [our] own salvation with fear and trembling . . ." the sole factor enabling us to do so is "God, who works in you, both to will and to work for his good pleasure" (Phil. 2:12–13). The entire divine priority in all phases of man's redemption, from eternity past to eternity future, is stoutly summarized in Romans 8. These verses contain what has been called "the chain of salvation":

> For those whom he foreknew he also predestined to be conformed to the image of his Son, in order that he might be the firstborn among many brothers. And those whom he predestined he also called, and those whom he called he also justified, and those whom he justified he also glorified.
>
> What then shall we say to these things? If God is for us, who can be against us? He who did not spare his own Son but gave him up for us all, how will he not also with him graciously give us all things? (Rom 8:29–32).

This passage shows that the unshakable assurance of our salvation originates *only* in God's gracious initiative. Here are the grand indicatives of our redemption, that is, the account of what God has already given us in Christ: our identity in Christ and the ensuing benefits of that union. These lofty indicatives facilitate our understanding of his commandments for us to have no other gods before his face, to serve him as our only Master, to seek first his kingdom and his righteousness, and to separate ourselves totally from the world (Ex. 20:3; Matt. 6:24, 33; James 4:4). In other words, *God's pre-existence of being and his initiative in creation and redemption are the logical and theological foundation for his requiring absolute obedience of his creatures.*

The Intrusion of Sin

The vicious intrusion of sin into the creation has permanently defiled and deranged the original, pristine relationship between God and man. It has torn Creator and creature so far apart and in such a manner that the restoration of their relationship is no longer possible without the divine initiative to interpose a Mediator, who must perfectly represent both God and man. Once more the *Westminster Confession* helps us grasp the graciousness of God in sovereignly establishing a second covenant, a covenant of grace, through which he freely offers eternal life to condemned, powerless sinners justly deserving death:

> Man, by his fall, having made himself incapable of life by that covenant, the Lord was pleased to make a second, commonly called the covenant of grace; wherein he freely offereth unto sinners life and salvation by Jesus Christ, requiring of them faith in him, that they may be saved; and promising to give unto all those that are ordained unto eternal life his Holy Spirit, to make them willing, and able to believe.[20]

Here we witness the sovereign God, the faultless, offended, and omnipotent party, taking the initiative to restore this fractured relationship. God, who would have yet been absolutely loving and merciful by leaving man to reap the just deserts of his cosmic treason, instead takes the first step in bringing the two parties together. The *Confession* here highlights the divine process for ensuring the salvation of the elect sinner, namely the monergistic regenerating work of the Holy Spirit enabling those ordained unto eternal life to willingly place their trust in Jesus Christ alone for salvation. Note the Trinitarian dimension of this redemption and note again that the context of this restorative initiative is a covenant, specifically the covenant of grace, sovereignly inaugurated in Genesis 3:15 and sovereignly administered until the second coming of Christ.

In summary, *the divine initiative in revelation and redemption constitutes the basis for all of God's dealing with his subjects.* Flowing from the very character of God, who is continuously condescending to reveal himself to his creatures by speaking and acting, this initiative is manifest in every step of both creation and redemption and, existentially, at every juncture of our lives in such a way that man is always reacting to the revelation that God has already given him in nature and in the person and work of Jesus Christ.

If these are the critical data concerning the meaning of *theology*, then what are we to understand by the larger term *biblical theology*?

What Is Biblical Theology?

At the risk of oversimplification, *biblical theology is the study of the self-revelation of God in the Bible from Genesis to Revelation*. As such, biblical theology takes an expansive, panoramic view of God's revelation of himself and his actions in biblical history. Consequently, it may be helpful if we summarize its main aspects.

Biblical theology can be summarized under the following main features[21]:

The Historic Progressiveness of the Revelation Process
God's revelation in history is a long series of continuous, unified acts covering all ages, nations, classes, and conditions of people. He has seen fit to unfold it in a sequence of words and acts, appearing and occurring over a long passage of time. God does not give his revelation in the form of a one-time, vast, unified block of history. Instead, he graciously accommodates the finiteness of human understanding by breaking it up into several stages (epochs), each of which is marked by successive covenant-makings. Each stage progresses with increasing clarity as in the gradual appearance of one ray of light after another.[22]

This historical divine self-revelation does not stand alone but is inseparably connected with divine redemption. God's revelation interprets his redemptive work, and its chief focus is the objective, central aspects of the person and work of Christ as seen in his incarnation, atonement, resurrection, and ascension. The application of Christ's work, that is, regeneration, justification, conversion, sanctification, and glorification are considered the subjective-individual aspect of redemption; they are extremely important but are not the chief concern of divine revelation.[23]

The Actual Embodiment of Revelation in History

God's acts of revelation are *really* his redeeming work, which attain highest significance in the atoning work of Jesus Christ. *God's specific acts, such as the redemption of his covenant people from Egypt and the crucifixion and resurrection of Christ,* are in fact *his Self-disclosure.* Even if there were no written Word to explain them, these acts would speak for themselves in a revelatory way and furnish both the foundation as well as the framework for a unified history of redemption.[24] The epitome of divine revelation is the historic substitutionary, sacrificial work of Jesus Christ on the cross at Calvary. Therefore, although redemption and revelation coincide, revelation is secondary to redemption and actually subserves it. God's redemptive acts are always preceded and followed by his revelatory Word in such an integrated, unifying manner that the "Old Testament brings the predictive, preparatory word" about Christ and his redemptive work, "the Gospels record these historical facts, and the Epistles offer their subsequent and final interpretation."[25]

In this way we witness the consoling truth that all of divine revelation and redemption is centered on Jesus Christ. As he himself rebuked the despairing disciples on their way to Emmaus:

> "O foolish ones, and slow of heart to believe all that the prophets have spoken! Was it not necessary that the Christ should suffer these things and enter into his glory?" And beginning with Moses and all the Prophets, he interpreted to them in all the Scriptures the things concerning himself (Luke 24:25–27).

He later re-affirmed this central truth as he appeared to the larger group of disciples:

> "These are my words that I spoke to you while I was still with you, that everything written about me in the Law of Moses and the Prophets and the Psalms must be fulfilled." Then he opened their minds to understand the Scriptures, and said to them, "Thus it is written, that

the Christ should suffer and on the third day rise from the dead, and that repentance and forgiveness of sins should be proclaimed in his name to all nations, beginning from Jerusalem" (Luke 24:44–47).

Biblical theology therefore helps us to recognize that Jesus Christ is the consistent, unifying element of Scripture. It is in his historical person and work that the unity of the Bible inheres. It is in him that all of Scripture finds its full and ultimate meaning. It is in him that the meaning and unity of all Scripture are concentrated, comprehended, and consummated. As another writer has stated, Christ is the goal of redemptive history, not merely the end of the process, and as such he forces us to understand the entire Bible in light of the gospel in which he is revealed.[26]

The Organic Nature of the Historic Process Is Seen in Revelation
Simply stated, God's self-revelation throughout all stages of history has been organically and essentially the same. The essential message of Scripture, namely, God's gracious provision of salvation to lost and condemned men of all ages and nationalities, through faith alone in Jesus Christ alone, is found in varying dimensions of maturity and clarity throughout the Bible. This seed of salvation, divinely implanted in the very beginning of Scripture, occurs in increasing clarity throughout the successive stages of revelation, gradually ripening and bearing new shoots, branches, and flowers along its divinely ordained path, until it finally bursts forth in its full soteric bloom at the consummation of the new covenant.[27] *Ultimately, therefore, this internally-driven organic progress has to do with God's introducing a new order in Christ into the fallen world.* All Scripture, from Genesis to Revelation, has its organic acids in the person and redemptive work of Jesus Christ. Though barely visible in the earliest writings, this organic essence is sufficiently present and visible in increasing clarity in the lives of the patriarchs, kings, and prophets, until it assumes its actual embodiment in Jesus Christ who ushers in its eschatological consummation.

The rich and various expressions of the organic progress of revelation do not conflict with or contradict one another but in fact demonstrate the unity and infallibility of Scripture (revelation), which is itself the supernaturally inspired, infallible Word of its rich and complex author, the sovereign God himself. The bottom line is that the inherently rich and multifaceted dimension of the infallible truth of Scripture reflects the very character of the God who authors it and whom it portrays. An infallible God will always present an infallible expression of his nature and purpose in every manner he condescends to make himself known.[28] Edmund Clowney summarizes this perspective by stating, "In tracing the progress of revelation, biblical theology rests upon the unity of the primary authorship of Scripture and the organic continuity of God's work in redemption and revelation."[29]

The Practical Adaptability of God's Revelation

God does not reveal himself to his creatures merely for intellectual purposes, but for them to get to know him. The truths of biblical theology are lived out in the lives of God's covenant people. For example, we do not understand history as a series of random acts but as the inexorable unfolding of the sovereign God's plans and purposes, which will attain their consummation in Christ. In other words, biblical theology informs and instructs us in every aspect of our lives.

The knowledge we obtain from biblical theology issues forth in an intimacy expressed in covenant loyalty. To this end, God, in his manifold wisdom, has freely chosen to interweave his revelation into every fiber and fabric of the lives of his elect so as to ensure its practical outworking in all its varied forms. Thus, the great news of this divine self-disclosure is that God did not reveal himself to his people in the context of a school, that is, in a manner of theoretical instruction, but rather in a covenant. Covenant living encompasses all of life.[30]

The Cosmic Dimension of the Historic, Organic Process

As stated earlier, the entire process of revelation has a cosmic dimension. It subserves the sovereign, divine purposes in redemption, the eternal center of which is Jesus Christ. Therefore, while it includes the personal dimension of the endowment of the individual with a new body like that of Christ (Phil. 3:21), it more so extends to the restoration of the entire universe from its fallen, mournful condition to an irenic splendor far exceeding that of the primeval garden in chapters 1 and 2 of Genesis. Old Testament redemption, portrayed in the impressive and elaborate sacrificial system, points to and foreshadows the coming Redeemer Messiah, who is progressively revealed at every juncture of the Old Testament dispensation. He is prefigured as the triumphant seed of the woman who will crush the head of the serpent (Gen. 3:15); as the Passover Lamb; as the center and focus of the entire Levitical priesthood with its attendant cultic practices; by the tabernacle in the wilderness and the temple in the Promised Land (both signifying the presence of the Lord among his people); as the subject of all the poetic and wisdom literature; as the subject of prophecy; and as the One who will redeem his people from their exile into sin.

This revelation reaches its apex in the incarnation of the God-man, Jesus Christ, who throughout his ministry on earth continually pointed to himself as the fulfillment of all that the entire Old Testament (which he variously designated as the Law and the Prophets, or as the law of Moses, the Prophets, and the Psalms) spoke (Luke 24:25–27, 44–47). This fulfillment attains its highest significance in his atoning sacrifice on the cross. His resurrection from the grave serves to vindicate every claim he made about himself and guarantees not only that all who are united to him through the unbreakable bond of the Holy Spirit will be resurrected as he was and will be further clothed with their new heavenly dwelling (2 Cor. 5:1–2), but also that the entire inanimate creation will receive its new redemptive clothing from him. Therefore, *Christ is our eschatological goal.* Through Christ and Christ alone, the Father will ultimately redeem both his chosen people and the heavens and earth that he created and affirmed with the divine benediction, "it is good," unto himself for his own eternal glory.

The initial intention of the divine, cosmic redemptive purposes is stated in Genesis 3:15 where, in the midst of the pronouncement of a curse upon the serpent, our merciful and gracious God assumes the initiative by interposing *enmity* between the woman and the

serpent and between their respective seed (singular in the immediate context but by theological and historical evidence, expanded
to the plural). This enmity has been gradually revealed throughout
Scripture to be personalized in the incarnate Jesus Christ. As shown
earlier, this redemptive purpose did not originate in history but in
eternity past, and therefore ultimately is the product of God's eternal
decree, or "the wise, free, and holy acts of the counsel of his will,
whereby, from all eternity, he hath, for his own glory, unchangeably
foreordained whatsoever comes to pass in time, especially concerning angels and men."[31]

Why is this important? Because this is the essence of biblical
theology, which studies the redemptive revelation of God's words
and deeds in eternity and in history. The conclusion is inescapable:
although all redemptive history has been rightly referred to as a
footnote of Genesis 3:15, and although this all-important text is the
first reference to God's redemptive purposes in history, the divine
purposes have their ultimate source in God's inerrant, inspired, and
infallible Word, immutably decreed in eternity past and gradually
substantiated in history.

The Testimony of Two Trees
The entire biblical theological approach to life can be seen from the
analogy of two crepe myrtle plants.

Years ago my wife, Mary, and I purchased two small crepe myrtles from one of the local garden stores. The trees were small, not
more than six inches in height, and our intent was to plant them
in the front of the yard. Above and against my prevailing doubts
concerning their survival, Mary assured me that they would grow
into huge plants that would actually provide beauty to our yard,
shade to our home, and value to our property. As we transplanted
the tiny plants from their confining plastic holders into their larger,
verdant surroundings, I could not help noticing how frail and helpless they were.

I feared their demise at the hands of the heavy rains that would
be soon pressing down with persistence. How could they withstand
the seemingly merciless southern heat that was due to appear in less

than two months? Above all, how could they escape the devouring blades of my lawnmower, which I was wont to direct in a fast and furious manner when my macho adrenaline was flowing? This latter concern proved to be proleptic, for three weeks after when I was waxing industriously, this galloping grass-eater accidentally clipped one of the little trees. Instinctively, I stopped, bent over, and, assuming the role of a professional horticulturalist, assiduously began to supply soothing restoration.

By the end of that year the darling plantlets had risen to about three feet in height. Their limbs were developing plant muscles and had begun to spread upward and outward. They survived a chilly but almost totally dry winter, and during the next year, their eager and elegant efflorescence continued with an amazing display of buds, blossoms, and brightness, all of which made them seem like plant peacocks strutting their stuff as they strove to gain the attention and admiration of dispassionate onlookers.

Twelve months later their bold growth was violently arrested by a vicious attack of Japanese beetles, rapacious insects that quickly transformed the promising young ones into a defoliated disaster. Their beautiful blossoms soon disappeared and the joyful, luscious leaves were disfigured into dark, dry, and brittle stems, easily breakable by a normal human encounter, much less an accidental meeting with a marauding lawnmower! I once more assumed the role of the resident redeemer, and following the advice of the owner of a nearby greenery, sprayed the struggling shrubs with the recommended grayish, pungent anti-beetle formula. A week later, I noticed that the beetles had died and that the leaves and limbs were regaining their verdant vigor. With the passage of another week, they were well on their way to a complete rejuvenation and were once again singing praises to the glory of God. The unevenly shaped pink blossoms were re-appearing at every level, and the branches had regained their swagger as they once more danced nimbly in the gentle summer wind.

Today, both plants are more than six feet in height and are spreading in width. Branches hardly sway when birds alight on them, and their increased robustness is continuously fostered by a three-dimensional growth—upward in height, outward in spread, and downward in root. What is even more outstanding is this: as I was driving through our subdivision in midsummer, I noticed two huge trees in one of our neighborhood's better-kept yards. Since I pass this way at least twice per day, I am sure that I had seen them on innumerable occasions. However, that day something stood out: the trees bore the same type of blossoms as ours. A closer look confirmed their shape and contour to be similar to the six-footers in our yard. These massive trees were higher than the telephone lines and were casting abundant shade around their home. They were crepe myrtles, of the same kind as the pretentious ones in our yard. In addition to my sheepish concession to Mary that she was right (one more time), I also marveled at the great possibility that our two trees, once so diminutive and delicate, could also ascend to such impressive heights, conceivably in my lifetime!

Obviously, this extensive episode on the existential challenges of a couple of crepe myrtles is not self-serving. This account is a vivid analogy of the growth of the kingdom of God as explained by the principles of biblical theology. While the parallels between the growth of the trees and the flow of redemptive history have some discontinuities (for example, crepe myrtle plants multiply their stems as they grow so that the trees do not have one sole, stout trunk as an oak or pine tree, but several that are held closely together), nevertheless the similitude is pressing. We will examine these from three perspectives.

Historicalness. This is patent. The life circumstances of the trees occurred in the continuum of time and history just as the events of divine redemption are revealed in Scripture. As redemptive history is true because it *is* God's speech and action concerning his self-revelation in creation and redemption, so the transactions of the plants are true primarily because they "are speaking" to us, that is, we see and "hear" their stubborn historicalness.

Progressiveness. The similarity between the development of the trees and that of redemptive history is also manifest. In both there is a gradual, discernible development from the lower to the higher, from the smaller to the bigger, from the unsophisticated to the sophisticated, and from the apparently insignificant to the undoubtedly significant. Both cases involve a sequence of development that, while linear in its due direction, occurs "through many dangers, toils and snares," requiring radical and critical external intrusions to ensure their teleological intent. For both, this superior *ab extra* involvement is necessary for their survival.

Organic Growth. Lastly, both plant and heavenly kingdom have the essential being inhering in them throughout every stage of their growth. As at their tiniest level an organic essence of crepe myrtleness existed in the trees, so also the redemptive essence was present at the initial point of the divine self-revelation. Both grow into what they essentially are; no transmutation is possible. Above all, both are predestined for a tremendous transformation at the eschatological consummation.

In the meantime, the crepe myrtles, as indeed all of animate non-human creation, though now increasing in strength and beauty, are continuously longing to be rid of the futility to which their Creator has subjected them on account of the fall of Adam. Yearning for the realization of their full, eschatological glory, which they will inherit when we the sons of God receive ours at the second coming of Christ, they seem to be urging us to hasten in our assigned work that the final kingdom may be realized soon. The apostle Paul describes this universal yearning as follows:

> For the creation waits with eager longing for the revealing of the sons of God. For the creation was subjected to futility, not willingly, but because of him who subjected it, in hope that the creation itself will be set free from its bondage to corruption and obtain the freedom of the glory of the children of God. For we know that the whole creation has been groaning together in the pains of childbirth until now (Rom. 8:19–22).

This longing is also the intense articulation of those that are born again in true righteousness and holiness. There is a united groaning or eschatological fullness between the inhuman and the human creatures:

> And not only the creation, but we ourselves, who have the firstfruits of the Spirit, groan inwardly as we wait eagerly for adoption as sons, the redemption of our bodies. For in this hope we were saved . . . (Rom. 8:23–24).

This glorious consummation occurs by the divine irruption of the new heavens and earth from above (Rev. 21:1–5), and is made possible only by the radical resurrection of Christ, of whom it is stated:

> [H]e is the head of the body, the church. He is the beginning, the firstborn from the dead, that in everything he might be preeminent. For in him all the fullness of God was pleased to dwell, and through him to reconcile to himself all things, whether on earth or in heaven, making peace by the blood of his cross (Col. 1:18–20).

It is through Christ's matchless person as the second Adam, his reconciling work on the cross, and his vindication by the Father, who resurrected him from the grave, that all creation, though distorted and corrupted by the fall, attains its highest end for which it was made. All land and life will then be totally transformed into an inexpressibly magnificent kingdom with blessings far exceeding those of the present stage and at levels far outstripping its pristine, pre-fallen condition. Until and unto that day, its organic growth continues.

Implications for Black Theological Thinking

What does all this mean for African-American Christians? Why should the predominantly black church embrace this biblical theological understanding?

Coupled with the need for a thoroughly sound theology is the requirement for us to see all life and experience, whether we perceive it as good or bad, as being decreed by God and as part of his sovereign control over our lives. The grand story of historical redemption discussed by biblical theology applies to all of God's creation without exception. It encompasses not only the major historical events in life but also the small, "insignificant" activities such as the invisible growth of a blade of grass in the sprawling rain forests of South America.

Slavery and Its Results

Among many black Christians the prevailing thought is that the unspeakable harshness and barbarism of slavery should spell equal consequences upon its wicked perpetrators. Some hearts are so callous that they cannot bring themselves to have any affinity whatsoever for whites. Among others, there is such an inbred indifference that for them, whites do not even exist; they have blotted them out emotionally, and no amount of physical closeness that comes from being coworkers, sharing the same public amenities, and encountering one another at local schools, grocery stores, or cinemas can change this. Whether the attitude is one of "they did it to us first" or "do unto them because they did it unto you," it demonstrates an obdurate unwillingness to forgive in the strength of Christ and in the manner that the Father has already forgiven us (Matt. 6:12; Eph. 4:32; Col. 3:13), that we may receive his continuing forgiveness (Matt. 6:14–15). Such a stance promotes and points to a lack of *shalom* (peace), the sense of integrated well-being within us.

In the context of our current discussion on biblical theology, such stubbornness points to a deficiency in understanding God's sovereign work of redemption. For one thing, it neglects the truth that God is sovereignly working all things for his eternal purposes, always moving and removing, placing and displacing, setting and upsetting all things and people, even royal potentates, according to his immutable purposes (Isa. 40:23–24). It is he, who

> hath all life, glory, goodness, blessedness, in and of himself; and is alone in and unto himself all-sufficient, not standing in need of any creatures which he hath made, nor deriving any glory from them, but only manifesting his own glory in, by, unto, and upon them. He is the alone fountain of all being, of whom, through whom, and to whom

are all things; and hath most sovereign dominion over them, to do by them, for them, or upon them whatsoever himself pleaseth. . . .[32]

Bearing these truths in mind and reflecting on our earlier thoughts on biblical theology, *it is both plausible and necessary to see the institution of slavery as one of the epochs used by God in furthering his gospel to the Gentiles, specifically, Africans.* It is part of his unquestionable, most holy, wise, and perfect divine plan to bring his great salvation to our people. In his most wise, sovereign, efficacious manner, he foreordains both the means and the end of all his purposes.

Divine Sovereignty and Human Accountability

What is the correct biblical perspective of slavery, racism, and many of the unjust systems and means used by man in subjecting his fellow man? First, we are to view them as sin. Being made in the image of God entails that man is a free, moral agent who is accountable to God. Man's actions are judged in light of God's standard of righteousness and justice. Second, we are to understand them from the perspective of Christ, who, concerning his impending betrayal by one of his followers, stated, "The Son of Man goes as it has been determined, but woe to that man by whom he is betrayed!" (Luke 22:22).

Here is the perfect balancing of the tension between divine sovereignty and human accountability. Our Lord Jesus is in fact saying that Judas would not be able to stand before him on the day of judgment and protest, "Lord, I fulfilled the plan of the Father to deliver you into the hands of your executioners just as he had ordained it. Since I was obedient to the heavenly vision, you should therefore let me enter into your heaven." Similarly, when Adam sinned against God, he could not declare that he was exempt from judgment because he had fulfilled his role in the divine decree of the fall; for that matter, neither could the serpent nor the woman. As was shown in the garden of Eden with the first sinners, the fact that God elects to use secondary causes in the execution of his eternal purposes does not absolve those agents from moral accountability to him. In his bold proclamation of the gospel in the book of Acts, the restored Peter declared, "This Jesus, delivered up according to the definite plan and foreknowledge of God, you crucified and killed by the hands of lawless men" (Acts 2:23). Two chapters later he again confirmed that:

> "The kings of the earth set themselves,
>   and the rulers were gathered together,
>   against the Lord and against his Anointed"—
>
> for truly in this city there were gathered together against your holy servant Jesus, whom you anointed, both Herod and Pontius Pilate, along with the Gentiles and the peoples of Israel, to do whatever your hand and your plan had predestined to take place (Acts 4:26–28).

In another place, the Scripture is even more graphic in describing the Father's intentionality in delivering the Son to be crucified, for "it was the will of the LORD to crush him; he has put him to grief" (Isa. 53:10).

These passages tell us that God's eternal decree concerning the predestinated crucifixion of Jesus necessarily entailed its execution in history by man. As a matter of fact, we may even say that *God's eternal decree establishes human involvement and accountability in their fulfillment.* By this we learn that the divine decree does not leave man in a cold and cruel predeterministic state, but implicates his free participation in such a way that, far from absolving him from any accountability to God, establishes and undergirds it. To be sure, this is a profound mystery, which in technical terms is described as an antinomy, an apparent contradiction between two equally valid evident truths. The presence of an antinomy in Scripture does not testify to any flaw therein, but rather illustrates the mysterious character of its author. The mystery of the incomprehensible God does not provoke our denunciation of his attributes but compels us to bow in fearful worship of this *mysterium tremendum.*

Our view of slavery and other oppressive events should therefore be, "As for you, you meant evil against me, but God meant it for good, to bring it about that many people should be kept alive, as they are today" (Gen. 50:20). As bitter as those experiences have been, and in many cases, still are, we must strive to see the sovereign, omnipotent hand of God behind them all. It was he who foreordained not only the good of our salvation but also the means by which it was to be achieved. Slavery took place just as our most wise, holy God foreordained it, but woe to those persons who executed it. The sinful participants in divine redemptive purposes cannot claim any absolution whatsoever for their sinful role in God's eternal enterprise but are held accountable to him for their sin.

Our View of Scripture

Constantly retaining a panoramic view of God's sovereign control over all of his creation also reinforces Scripture's view of itself as God's objective self-revelation that he breathed out and caused to be supernaturally, inerrantly, and infallibly inscripturated in a unified, coherent, and organic manner by human authors. When we approach the biblical text therefore, we are to see it as the very Word of God, the record of the progressive unfolding of his purposes, internally consistent and self-verifying by the application of its self-evident principle that Scripture interprets Scripture (the *analogy of faith*). This perspective guards us against the errors of proof-texting and atomistic exegesis, for it helps us to verify the meaning of particular texts from the meaning of other Scriptures and also from Scripture as a whole. It also undergirds us against a hermeneutic of suspicion, that is, distrust in the Bible simply because others have perverted it to fulfill their sinister ends. Finally, it requires us to come to the Scripture to discover its inherent truth and not to construct "our truth." This latter point has utmost significance for many blacks who, while correctly rejecting older distortions of Scripture advanced to justify racial oppression, have sought to establish their own paradigms of interpretation. *The regrettable outcome is that many of us have subjectively made the African-American experience the center of biblical emphasis.*[33] In this scenario, the African-American experience, not the person and work of Christ, becomes the paradigm for interpreting and understanding Scripture. This undermines biblical authority rather than strengthening it.

Biblical Theology and Worship, Preaching, and Sanctification

How does biblical theology relate to the other topics of this work?

Worship

Biblical theology enhances our understanding of the soteriological dimension of worship. It enables us to acknowledge that we are part of the historical, progressive, organic divine drama, that we are players and actors on the stage, God himself being the main actor. As his covenant people, we respond joyfully to the great privilege of being counted as his redeemed. Our election before the foundation of the world has bestowed this status upon us. We are delighted to be his redeemed covenant community, to be "a chosen race, a royal priesthood, a holy nation, a people for his own possession," whom God has transported, transferred, and transformed from the kingdom "of darkness into his marvelous light," for his own glory, that we might proclaim his excellencies (1 Pet. 2:9). That we are the unworthy recipients of this divine favor should flood our hearts and warm our souls with joyful gratitude at all times but especially when we are corporately assembled in his presence to worship him.

In worship we recall that we are his people, his own inheritance for whom he is jealous. In worship we are reminded that it is he who has adopted us into his royal family and that we are pilgrims making our progress to our final destination, heaven, where we will be with him forever. This comforting anticipation hovers before, around, and within us and garrisons our hearts and minds as our strong consolation, encouragement, and hope.

In worship, we continually confirm its soteriological context and content as we are gathered *coram Deo,* literally, "before the face of God." We graciously recount our covenant solidarity and covenant succession with Israel, who, when assembled in God's holy presence at Mount Sinai to be constituted as his covenant community, were waiting to receive instructions for their daily lives from him who had just delivered them from the oppressive enemy. Like Israel, we repeatedly ask ourselves, what does this redemption of God mean? What is its ongoing significance? What are its continuing implications for our lives? Just as Israel made a vow before the Lord, saying, "All that the Lord has spoken we will do, and we will be obedient" (Ex. 24:7), so we make holy vows to him in worship. Just as Israel partook of a covenantal, sacramental meal commemorating her epochal redemption from her chief enemy, we likewise participate in the Lord's Table (Luke 22:15–20), Christ's perpetual ordinance commemorating his death by which he redeemed us unto himself, until the time of his second coming when we will eternally partake of the wedding supper of the Lamb (Rev. 19:1–6).

Just as Israel was baptized into Moses as they fled from Pharaoh, we likewise are baptized into Christ, the Mediator of the new and better covenant. In worship, as we are assembled on Mount Zion, we look back and trace our covenant union with Israel, the prototypical assembly, but we also look forward to our eternal assembly in heaven and to our eternal serendipity with our God. We stand between the past and the future assemblies participating in both, joined by our union in Christ and looking forward to worshiping him forever and ever.

Preaching

Biblical theology constantly reminds us of both the content and the context of preaching. We affirm that the content of preaching is the cross of Christ. Paul specifically explains that, whereas the Jews demand a sign, and the Greeks pursue wisdom, "we preach Christ crucified, a stumbling block to Jews and folly to Gentiles," (1 Cor. 1:22). At other times he uses the synonymous phrase "preach the gospel" (Rom. 1:15; 15:20; 1 Cor. 1:17–18; 2 Cor. 2:12; 10:16). This preaching of the gospel is so self-emptying that it affords us no ground for boasting. As a matter of fact, Paul feels the burden of this accountability so much that he even invokes a self-imprecatory pronouncement (1 Cor. 9:16) should he be unfaithful in his calling. As if this were not enough, he intensifies the consequences of unfaithfulness in preaching by the pronouncement of an anathema or curse upon those preaching another gospel (Gal. 1:8–9).

Through preaching, the continuation of the dialogue from God to man in God's assembled covenant community, biblical theology reminds us that we are part of the historical, progressive, organic process of God's redemption. It buttresses the point that, not only are we the continuing, historical people of God "occupying a particular place in the plan of the ages, that is, in the history of redemption," but also that we are an eschatological people, a people "on whom the end of the ages has come" (1 Cor. 10:11).[34] While our forefathers anticipated the coming of the Messiah, we, unto whom the sovereign Lord has been pleased to grant a complete self-revelation in the person and work of Jesus Christ, also stand in line of this anticipation, although it is not the first but the second coming of our Lord Jesus Christ that we seek. "No racial memory, no cultural tradition, no transmission of religious experience, nothing that is of man and by men could account for the radical continuity of revelation which we find in the Scriptures."[35]

Preaching that is true to biblical theology therefore impresses this organic continuity of redemptive history upon the hearts and minds of its hearers, whom it comforts with joyful reminders of their unconditional election by and unto the Father for his own glory. It continually seeks to remind us that Jesus Christ is the hermeneutical apex of all Scripture (Luke 24:25–27, 44–47).

Lastly, our preaching is to reflect this entire objective aspect of God's self-realization in history. It must constantly drive home the unity of Scriptures in such a way that the Old Testament is not reduced to a collection of writings providing us with awe-inspiring biographies, gripping military episodes, and encouraging ethical examples. How often have we come across Sunday school or vacation Bible school materials limiting Joseph to a victimized, godly young man, rejected and spurned by even his loved ones! How many times have we read stories that restrict the life of Daniel to a good example for us to emulate in the face of peer pressure! Have we not frequently heard Mordecai's famous statement to Esther, "and who knows whether you have not come to the kingdom for such a time as this?" used to manipulate women to teach a Sunday school class or to volunteer for nursery duty? Preaching that is faithful to biblical theology cites the Old Testament as the first part of God's unfolding cosmic redemptive plan, a plan that reaches its maturity in the once-for-all substitutionary atoning sacrifice of Jesus Christ.

Sanctification

A sound biblical theology helps us to recognize the proactive God working effectually in the lives of his elect in order that they will persevere in (their) faith until the end when he sends his Son to gather them in his presence in eternity.[36] Therefore, we are confident that whatever our situation in this life may be, we have the "unspeakable comfort" of knowing that it is God himself who has chosen us and separated us from the world unto himself. This divine election, being entirely of his free grace, necessarily places certain covenant obligations upon us. Just as Israel in the old covenant was required to be holy unto their Redeemer God because he is holy and because he redeemed them (Lev. 11:44–45; 19:2; 20:26), so also we of the new covenant are required to be holy according to the character of our Savior. To this end, Peter instructs his scattered and oppressed readers, "As obedient children, do not be conformed to the passions of your former ignorance, but as he who called you is holy, you also be holy in all your conduct, since it is written, 'You shall be holy, for I am holy'" (1 Pet. 1:14–16).

Yet, the Lord does not weigh us down with burdensome rules. His commands are always preceded by his empowering assurances of our status in Christ. In mildly technical language, this principle is known as the indicative of the gospel preceding the imperatives of the gospel. It is a typical covenant formula classically shown in Exodus 20:1–2 (the covenant preamble and prologue) where the Lord introduces himself to Israel and reminds them of his gracious redemption. Upon this basis, he delineates the stipulations they are to uphold (see Ex. 20:3–17).

Though we may from time to time succumb to temptation and spend many dark nights in the valley of Achor, we are comforted to know that God has predestined us unto holiness. He also graciously provides us with the existential promise that after we have suffered a little while, joy will come in the morning.

The Pauline affirmation, "even as he chose us in him before the foundation of the world, that we should be holy and blameless before him" (Eph. 1:4), accompanies the opening paean of praise to the Triune God, "who has blessed us in Christ with every spiritual blessing in the heavenly places" (Eph. 1:3). From these verses we learn that not only does God intend for us to be holy but also that he equips us and grants us holy lives. He graciously works in our lives "both to will and to work for his good pleasure," and he constantly reminds us that "he who began a good work in you will bring it to completion at the day of Jesus Christ" (Phil. 2:13; 1:6). That is to say, *predestinating grace is a sanctifying grace,* a condition that is granted us by our union with Christ. The free grace of our redemption does not cause us to live lawlessly so that the more we sin the more God's grace may abound unto us. Rather, the grace we have received from the Father reigns in righteous living and leads to eternal life through our Lord Jesus Christ (Rom. 5:21). As the apostle Paul has instructed:

> We were buried therefore with him by baptism into death, in order that, just as Christ was raised from the dead by the glory of the Father, we too might walk in newness of life.
>
> For if we have been united with him in a death like his, we shall certainly be united with him in a resurrection like his (Rom. 6:4–5).

Biblical theology also reminds us that although our union in Christ grants us a *status* of absolute perfection before God, *experientially* our lives are progressively growing in holiness. As God continues to instruct us from his unfolding revelation, his indwelling sanctifying Spirit enables us to respond to him in such a way that shapes and molds us more and more to be what we were predestined to be, namely, ethically perfect, a condition that will be attained only in heaven. For this reason, a sound biblical theological perspective helps us to recognize that *sanctification therefore is ethical in content and eschatological in scope.* It is a process by which God is making us fit to be in his presence where there is no sin, hatred, sexual immorality, or any other form of evil forever (1 Cor. 6:9–10; Gal. 5:21;

Rev. 21:8). Sanctification therefore depicts the telic design of our redemption: *already* we are standing before God definitively perfect in Christ, but experientially we have *not yet* attained the fullness of our redemption. In short, our sanctification is "the cultivation of those . . . religious concerns" that are so inseparably joined with our eternal destiny.[37]

As you contemplate the remaining pages of this work, may the Lord God grant you a unifying perspective of the presence of his hand not only within the confines of this book but also in the entire realm of his creation and redemption. May you be encouraged in knowing that you are a part of his unified, historical, organic redemptive purposes that he established before he created the world, that he is even now unfolding, and that reaches its consummation in the person and work of Jesus Christ. The greatest comfort of all lies in the divinely established principle that all of his works are done *soli Deo gloria*, to the glory of God alone.

3

BIBLICAL PREACHING
Experiencing the Word of God

by ANTHONY J. CARTER

There is a familiar story about a young man who wanted to be a preacher. He had seen many fine preachers and thought it would be wonderful to be able to preach to people and have them respond with "amens" and "yes suhs." He sincerely believed that God had called him to be a preacher. He convinced the pastor and the deacons at his church to allow him to demonstrate this calling by affording him the opportunity to preach. Though they were weary of his giftedness and had their doubts about his understanding of this "call," they nevertheless gave him opportunity to preach one Sunday evening.

The young man gave it his best shot. But from the onset it was obvious that his heart was willing but the gift was not present. The people lovingly indulged his efforts with an occasional "amen" here and there, but everyone was relieved when he closed in prayer.

Nevertheless, the young man was encouraged by what he thought was a stellar performance. He subsequently spoke to the pastor about the possibility of future opportunities. The pastor, wondering how he might break the news to the young man that another opportunity was not going to be given, suggested to the young man that maybe another calling, perhaps Sunday school teacher or even deacon, was in his future. The young man would have no talk of it. He was convinced that God had called him and insisted that God had given him the gift of preaching. The pastor, frustrated by and weary of the boy's insistence, remarked, "Well, he may have given you the gift of preaching, but he has not given anyone else the gift of listening."

The predominantly black church in America has been a great assessor of preaching ability. Very few young men with any promise at public oration have escaped the church's attempts of getting them to the pulpit. Subsequently, very few black churches have lacked for men with speaking ability. No, the predominantly black church has not lacked men with style; what has been lacking, however, is substance. We have not been in need of better technique, but we have been in need of content—theological, biblical content.

Here is where Reformed theology could have it most important and influential impact upon the predominantly African-American church. Oh, that men with preaching ability would be informed with biblical theology! The world would see a church that it has rarely seen, and Satan would see a church that he would fear.

When I was in seminary, it became evident early on that the preaching classes offered were not going to be very useful to me. These classes spent most of the time teaching *how* to preach. I didn't go to seminary to learn how to preach, as much as I went to seminary to learn *what* to preach. Tony Evans, pastor of Oak Cliff Bible Fellowship in Dallas makes the point, "Black clergymen need exposure to biblical study, not to make us preachers, for such we already are, but to make us *better* preachers."[1] You see, in the predominantly African-American church, preaching is more caught than taught. Cleophus LaRue, author of the *Heart of Black Preaching*, has remarked:

In many white churches one is declared fit to preach through certification. In the black church one is declared fit to preach through demonstration. In the former you have to show that you have been appropriately exposed to the fundamentals of preaching. While in the latter you have to show that you actually have some proficiency in the preaching act itself.[2]

I am convinced that good preachers are born, not made. Seminaries and preaching and public speaking books may be able to teach a young man communication skills, inflection techniques, and hand gestures, but preaching is a gift bestowed by God. In other words, either you got it or you don't. The historic black church has been rather successful in identifying those who have it and those who don't. Nevertheless, being able, that is, having the gifts and the skills to orate, is not all that is necessary for success in preaching. True success is tied not only to style, but substance. There should be theological content to go along with technique and conduct. Enter Reformed theology.

Theology Drives Our Preaching

Every preacher is a theologian. Traditionally among African-Americans, it has been thought that theological training was destructive to good preaching. Such thinking has lead to the seemingly ubiquitous reference to "seminaries" as "cemeteries." There is the insinuation that going to seminary has killed more good preachers than it has developed. Unfortunately, there is some truth to most cultural axioms. And this one is no different. Too many young men have gone off to seminary with a burning and a zeal for the Bible and faithful preaching, only to have some bright-minded, self-intoxicated, rarely-believing, and barely-breathing seminary professor wrench from him the belief and zeal for God's Word. Too many young men have gone to seminary alive, only to leave it dead and confused. Consequently for many in the church, seminary has become a place for the spiritually dead, with theology being seen as its most potent form of cyanide.

One young minister, whose pastor had received extensive seminary training at one of the more liberal institutions, suggested to me that his pastor had too much theology, and that he was leery of such training. I expressed to this young man two things. First, his pastor did not have too much theology. While theoretically that may be possible, I have yet to meet the person who has too much theology—too much knowledge of God. Second, the issue with his pastor was probably not that he had too much theology, but that he had bad theology.

The problem is not theology. The problem is bad, glory-bankrupt, corrupt, humanistic theology this is so popular in mainline seminaries and in popular charismatic, prosperity, mega-church pulpits. The bad theology is developed by the preacher, gets expressed in the preaching, and makes for bad (though sometimes entertaining) preaching. The preacher who preaches bad theology is a bad theologian. Every sermon is an expression of some theology. So the question is not whether a preacher is a theologian. Rather the question is, will he be a good theologian or a bad one? The only question is whether the theology being preached will be biblical, nonbiblical, or extra-biblical.

Our theology drives our preaching. It always has and it always will. The nature of one's theology designs the nature of one's preaching. For example, those who have a high view of God, that is, those who emphasize his transcendence or his separateness from his creation, will tend to have a higher, more thoughtful and intellectually driven approach to preaching. Their sermons tend to be delivered with more care to accuracy, because God's character is always at stake. When asked about the attention to preciseness in their preaching, these preachers will likely answer, "We are precise in our preaching because we have a precise God." The theology of God's character and attributes drives this preaching, and thus it informs the manner in which the preaching is done.

On the other hand, those who focus upon the immanence of God, namely his touching and involvement in his creation, will tend toward a more common reflection upon God and his people. Their sermons often will be viewed as more down-to-earth, using more common language and being more practical in their application. Their sermons will tend to be more emotionally and less intellectually driven, focusing not so much on the character of God as on the hand of God interacting with his creation. When asked about the practicality of their sermons, these preachers will likely respond, "We are practical in our preaching because God has given us a practical word in the Bible." The nearness of God and God's involvement in the lives of his people drives this preaching.

Another theological perspective that has driven preaching has been experiential theology. In fact, this has been the dominant perspective of the predominantly African-American church. Without a doubt, the history of African-American preaching has been that of an experientially driven proclamation. According to homiletics professor Cleophus LaRue, "the common threads of the oral tradition, black lived experience, and a shared history of subjugation undergird and sustain this tradition."[3] In experiential preaching, the preacher not only preaches what he has learned, but preaches what he has lived. This gives the preacher and the congregation a connection that is often manifested throughout the preaching event. The preacher is able to call upon a commonality of experience to which the congregation readily identifies. Mix this with exceptional oratory skills and you have the excitement that is often generated in the predominantly African-American church when the preacher is preaching.

It is no accident that the black church in America has tended to be more experientially driven than others, just as it is no accident that the major predominantly white denominations have been more intellectually driven. The majority of African-American churches are experientially driven due in large part to the experiential nature of the preaching. Emotions in preaching, as in life, play an important role in the effectiveness of our tradition. Concerning the need for an understanding of the experiential quality of black preaching, Evans states:

> Black preaching is thirsty for zest. And the black congregation will demand this zest. If there is not lively, earthy appeal in the sermon, it can become difficult to preach to a black congregation. And you cannot be a black preacher and not preach.[4]

Those who have been blessed to have been exposed to this experiential nature of preaching can truly cherish it. I have found it more refreshing even as it has challenged me to be more articulate and engaging in my preaching. I have found that experiential preaching can be just as biblically faithful as divine transcendence and divine immanence preaching can be. Biblical preaching, as in biblical theology, indeed proclaims the transcendence of God (Isa. 55:9) and proclaims the immanence of God (Acts 17:25, 28). Yet both find their ultimate expression when we experientially relate to the Lord Jesus Christ who has reconciled all things (transcendence and immanence) through his cosmic changing work on the cross (Col. 1:15–20).

Thus, to write of a Reformed experiential preaching in the African-American context is not as foreign as some may believe. As I argued in a previous work, Reformed theology is very compatible with the African-American experience.[5] Likewise, Reformed theology is compatible with African-American experiential preaching. In fact, if we understand Reformed experiential preaching, we will see that it has been what African-American churches have been used to hearing for centuries.

Reformed Experiential Preaching

In *Feed My Sheep: A Passionate Plea for Preaching*, Joel Beeke makes the case for experiential preaching. He defines experiential preaching as "preaching [that] seeks to explain in terms of biblical truth how matters ought to go, how they do go, what is the goal of the Christian life."[6] Experiential preaching seeks to examine everyday life in light of the Word of God. It also seeks to make the Word of God applicable to everyday life. Along these lines, Beeke further describes experiential preaching as *discriminatory preaching*:

> It clearly defines the difference between a Christian and non-Christian, opening the kingdom of heaven to one and shutting it against the other. Discriminatory preaching offers the forgiveness of sins and eternal life to all who by true faith embrace Christ as Savior

and Lord, but it also proclaims the wrath of God and his eternal condemnation upon those who are unbelieving, unrepentant, and unconverted.[7]

But not only is experiential preaching discriminatory, according to Beeke, it is also *applicatory preaching*:

> It applies the text to every aspect of a listener's life, promoting a religion that is truly a power and not mere form (2 Tim. 3:5). Robert Burns defined such religion as "Christianity brought home to men's business and bosoms," and said the principles on which it rests is "that Christianity should not only be known, and understood, and believed, but also felt, and enjoyed, and practically applied."[8]

Beeke makes a solid case for experiential preaching. Yet, in reading him I could not help but think that the predominantly black church in America has been the beneficiary of experiential preaching since its humble beginnings. The preaching that has traditionally long informed the pulpits in predominantly black churches has had many of the elements laid out by Beeke. In fact, some of the best experiential preaching the church has ever seen has been from black pulpits.

The genius of "black preaching" has been its ability to move, inspire, challenge, and motivate its listeners though stirring, rhetorical devises such as storytelling, song-singing, alliteration of points, the common use of language, and the lofty use of words. Even the ubiquitous "whoop" or "whooping" was (and is) employed regularly with the end of demonstrating the inherent experiential nature of the preaching event. The preacher does all he can to make the people not simply hear the Word of God, but experience the Word of God. And this experience is not simply religious experience, but it has been a social and even economic and political experience as well. The black preacher rarely draws back from examining every area of life. If experiential preaching is preaching to the "whole person," then none could deny that historic black preaching fits the bill. But simply having experiential preaching is not enough. Experiential preaching needs to be informed not with experience alone, but with biblically-faithful, Christ-centered, God-glorifying theology. In other words, it should be *Reformed* experiential preaching.

I love good black preaching. I love Reformed theology. I love when both of them come together. I believe it is the best the church has to offer. Yet before we offer some theological and practical ways in which this can happen, let us first briefly define what preaching is.

What Is Preaching?

Preaching is proclamation. It is the proclamation of calling men and women to behold Christ and the revelation of his kingdom come to earth through the preaching of the cross. It is the proclamation of this good and awesome news in a bad and awful world. The preacher then is a herald; he heralds the coming of Christ's kingdom and the multifaceted ways in which his people are called to display his rule. In short, preaching is the proclamation (heralding) of the kingdom of God.

The Scriptures demonstrate this early on in the New Testament revelation. When the first prominent New Testament preacher was heard, he was heard proclaiming, "Repent, for the kingdom of heaven is at hand" (Matt. 3:2). Jesus himself reminded us that preaching is heralding the presence of the kingdom. Upon his entering into public ministry, Jesus proclaimed, "Repent, for the kingdom of heaven is at hand" (Matt. 4:17).

The preacher who would be faithful to his calling would be the preacher who preaches the coming of the King and his kingdom. It will not matter what the particular subject or issue the text addresses, the preacher must proclaim the truth of the text in light of the fact that the kingdom of God is at hand. This was the charge Jesus gave to his disciples before he ascended.

In Matthew 28:18–20 we are given some of Jesus' last words to his disciples. He gives them their marching orders:

> And Jesus came and said to them, "All authority in heaven and on earth has been given to me. Go therefore and make disciples of all nations, baptizing them in the name of the Father and of the Son and

of the Holy Spirit, teaching them to observe all that I have commanded you. And behold, I am with you always, to the end of the age."

Clearly, Jesus was reminding his disciples that he was King, the one who has power and authority to rule over all. In light of this, their message was to make his kingdom known by declaration, disciple-making, and baptism. They were to proclaim the King and his kingdom. The charge has never changed. We are to preach the King and his kingdom. We are to preach his power and authority to rule on earth and in heaven.

The power of Jesus is inherent. In other words, Jesus did not derive his power, but power and authority has always been his. He had power and authority before the incarnation. He had power and authority throughout the time of his incarnation. And his power and authority was unchanged after his death and resurrection. What we see in the death and resurrection of Jesus is an unqualified and unequalled demonstration of that power and authority, whereby all creation must acknowledge that he is King. And thus we preach Christ—but not just Christ. We preach Christ and him crucified and ourselves as his subjects (1 Cor. 1:23; 2 Cor. 4:5). Christ is the essence and source of the kingdom and the substance of what we preach.

Though most Christians would agree that preaching Christ is the objective of faithful pulpit ministry, there remains a lack of the experiential reality of this truth. The truth is, Christ is not preached. This is due in large part to the fact that the content and theology of much of today's preaching is not Christ-centered or cross-centered. Preaching today is more style than substance; it is more character than content. The reclamation of Reformed thought and theology could turn this state of affairs around—particularly the reclamation of the five *solas* in our preaching.

Preaching and Preaching "Alones"

In writing this chapter I did not want to focus on the style of preaching. There are a plethora of preaching books that demonstrate adequately the various and effective forms of preaching today. Whether it is the expository sermon or the topical message, the declarative sermon or the narrative one, there are many books that describe the pros and cons of each of these approaches and will serve you well in discovering your most faithful approach.

My approach is not so much how we should preach, but what we should preach. The content of our sermons should be foremost, even before the form in which we bring them. Our preaching needs to be theologically sound. The form may vary and the audience may change, but the theological content must stay consistent. There must be a biblical theology that undergirds the form. Preaching that is theologically sound is preaching that is fenced in by what has historically been known as the *five* solas *of the Reformation.*

During the Reformation, the Protestant church developed five key phrases that defined the biblical faith. These five phrases have since served as a rallying cry for biblical Christianity. They are *sola Scriptura* (Scripture alone), *solus Christus* (Christ alone), *sola fide* (faith alone), *sola gratia* (grace alone), and *soli Deo gloria* (glory to God alone). These five phrases are not the sum total of the Christian faith, but they can serve as a worthy reminder and adequate guideline for the content of our preaching. One of the glorious ways in which the light of biblical truth could shine upon the Christian pulpit in general and the African-American pulpit in particular would be for the light of the Reformation to be recovered in our pulpits. This could principally be done through a conscious consideration of the five *solas* in our preaching. Biblical, Reformed, experiential preaching will take all them into account. To do so faithfully can do nothing but enhance and strengthen the preacher and congregation.

Sola Scriptura: The Light of the Word
The first of the five *solas* is *sola Scriptura* or "Scripture alone." Put simply this phrase means that the Bible is the sole source of written divine revelation. It means that the Scriptures are divinely inspired and as such are inerrant and infallible. The Scriptures are the final authority on and contain all that is necessary for biblical saving faith and godly living. The Bible states it this way: "All Scripture is

breathed out by God and profitable for teaching, for reproof, for correction, and for training in righteousness" (2 Tim. 3:16).

Biblical, experiential preaching begins with a commitment to the Bible as the Word of God. The preacher who would have any long-term credibility will be the preacher who consistently demonstrates that the Bible is the source of divine revelation and information. It is the place where he derives his authority and the place where his authority is checked.

Historically, African-Americans have believed the Bible to be the Word of God. Even today, as the idea of ultimate authority is eroding and ideas of absolute truth are widely dismissed, African-Americans generally believe that truth is not relative and the Bible is authoritative.

George Barna and Harry Jackson discovered that African-Americans have a higher view of the Scriptures than any other demographic in America. According to Barna and Jackson, when it comes to " 'active faith'—that is, people who attend church, read the Bible and pray during a given week," blacks surpass other groups in this regard.[9] Furthermore, "a huge majority of blacks (85 percent) contend that their religious faith is very important in their lives and that most black adults (60 percent) are convinced that the Bible is accurate in all of its teachings."[10] When we are speaking of preaching among blacks in America, our task is similar to that of the apostle Paul on Mars Hill in Athens where he said to those gathered before him, "Men of Athens, I perceive that in every way you are very religious" (Acts 17:22). Indeed, the numbers remind us today that we preach to a people who are very religious and have received a steady diet of religious language and symbols. And yet, as in Paul's day, being religious does not equate with a knowledge of the true and living God. On the contrary, that knowledge comes only by hearing, understanding, and experiencing the Word of God. To the extent that we are committed as preachers to the trustworthiness and incomparable ability of the Word of God to change our world is the extent to which we will see real reform. But it starts with our commitment to *sola Scriptura*.

Reform within the church has always begun with a recommitment to the Bible as the Word of God. In our day, it will be no different. And if the numbers are correct, bringing such reform to the predominantly black church may not be as difficult as one might think. Yet it must begin with faithful preaching that understands and promotes Scripture alone as its principal source.

Unfortunately, many Christians treat their Bible as they would their local newspaper, because they have been taught to do so by their preachers. The faithful preacher, however, understands the Bible differently. A newspaper is a composite of many parts and sections. There is the front page, the business section, the sports page, the living and entertainment section, and so on. All of these sections make up the one newspaper. And yet, no section is actually dependent upon the other. A person can read the sports page and completely understand the issues and concerns of the day in sports without ever looking at the front page. Likewise a person can read the entertainment section and understand it fully with little to no knowledge of the goings on in sports. The Bible is no such book. And to preach under the rubric of *sola Scriptura* is to understand this.

The Bible is indeed a collection of sixty-six separate writings. A person could indeed read one of the sections of the writings and get a sense of what is happening without much knowledge of other sections. However, that same person would never really know what any section of Scripture was communicating unless that person were interested in knowing how that particular section fits into the grand, overall picture the Bible is painting.

More than a newspaper, the Bible is a literary portrait. The subject of the portrait is Christ. Each division of the Bible adds something important and indispensable to the portrait. And while a person may be able to make out the picture without all the sections together, what a glorious experience it is when one sees all the sections fitting together! This is the role of the artist. This is the calling of the preacher. He is to show that the Bible, from cover to cover, is painting a picture of Christ. He is to show how each part of the painting is interrelated. And whether he is preaching from Revelation or John or

Leviticus, he is to demonstrate how that section fits into the display of the glorious whole, namely the revelation of Jesus Christ.

This will demonstrate the overall cohesiveness of the Bible and the perspicuity of the Scriptures. It will also develop in people the sense of the high place the Word of God has in the life and living of the church. It will quickly become the place where people turn when life and living need answers.

Solus Christus: The Light of Christ

The next of the five solas is *solus Christus* or "Christ alone." This means that in Christ alone is the efficacious work of redemption accomplished on our behalf. His sinless life and vicarious death have become our portion, and through him alone we have justification and reconciliation with God. Christ's life and death are sufficient alone to accomplish satisfaction, substitution, and sanctification on the behalf of sinners. The substance of the gospel in found in the person and work of Christ. Subsequently, in Christ alone we have the forgiveness of sins (Col. 1:13–14). The Bible declares the sufficiency of Christ when it says, "For Christ also suffered once for sins, the righteous for the unrighteous, that he might bring us to God, being put to death in the flesh but made alive in the spirit" (1 Pet. 3:18).

To preach biblically faithful sermons is to preach Christ. It is to preach Christ in all his fullness. It is proclaiming the impeccable life and substitutionary death of Christ. It is proclaiming his glorious resurrection, his righteous and royal ascension, and his ever-priestly, ongoing ministry.

Graeme Goldsworthy asked the question, "Can I preach a Christian sermon without mentioning Jesus?" The question seems an odd one since "Christian" literally means "belonging to Christ." And yet in our modern age of downplaying and even questioning the uniqueness of Christ, it is an important question. It is a question that every faithful preacher must ask and answer. Goldsworthy rightly points us to Christ for the answer:

> If we would see God, he is most clearly revealed in Jesus Christ. If we would see what God intends for our humanity, it is most clearly

revealed in Jesus Christ. If we would see what God intends for the created order, we discover that it is bound up with our humanity and, therefore, revealed in Christ. While the temptation in preaching will be strong to proceed directly from, say, the godly Israelite to the contemporary believer, this method will inevitably produce distortions in the way we understand the text. There is no direct application apart from the mediation of Christ . . . we simply can not afford to ignore the words of Jesus that the Scriptures testify to him.[11]

The apostle Paul has given every preacher his marching orders in 1 Corinthians 1:23: "We preach Christ. . . ." We are not to preach around Christ, but Christ. We are not to suggest Christ, but rather proclaim him. We are not simply to admire Christ, but rather preach Christ. And why? Because Christ is our wisdom, righteousness, sanctification, and redemption (1 Cor. 1:30). He is our all, and so we preach Christ.

John Calvin summed up this cardinal doctrine with this wonderful admonition:

We see that our whole salvation and all its parts are comprehended in Christ (Acts 4:12). We should therefore take care not to derive the least portion of it from anywhere else. If we seek salvation, we are taught by the very name of Jesus that it is "of him" (1 Cor. 1:30). If we seek any other gifts of the Spirit, they will be found in his anointing. If we seek strength, it lies in his dominion; if purity, in his conception; if gentleness, it appears in his birth. For by his birth he was made like us in all respects (Heb. 2:17), that he might learn to feel our pain (cf. Heb. 5:2). If we seek redemption, it lies in his passion; if acquittal, in his condemnation; if remission of the curse, in his cross (Gal. 3:13); if satisfaction, in his sacrifice; if purification, in his blood; if reconciliation, in his descent into hell; if mortification of the flesh, in his tomb; if newness of life, in his resurrection; if immortality in the same; if inheritance of the Heavenly Kingdom, in his entrance into heaven; if protection, if security, if abundant supply of all blessings, in his Kingdom; if untroubled expectation of judgment, in the power given to him to judge. In short, since rich store of every kind of good abounds in him, let us drink our fill from this fountain, and from none other.[12]

Indeed, let us not only drink from this fountain alone, but let us preach from it alone as well.

Sola Fide: The Light of Faith

The third of the *solas* is *sola fide* or "faith alone." This doctrine simply means that the work of Christ in his living and his dying is a work that is received and accounted to the sinner by faith and nothing else. The sinner who is received by God and is judged as righteous and thus is no longer under the condemnation for his sin is the sinner who has received Christ and has had the righteousness of Christ made over unto him. The receiving and accounting is done by faith in Christ and nothing else.

The call of the preacher is to preach so the sinner might know the way to heaven—the way into the kingdom now and forever. Modern preaching is so occupied with the now that it almost completely misses the reason for Christ's coming into the world. He died that we might live (1 Thess. 5:9–10). Yes, his death does secure for us life now, but that is but a by-product of life everlasting. Most preaching today is full of practical steps to live a wealthier and healthier American life. There is little thought of the Bible's overwhelming preoccupation with eternity. The question is not, how can I stand more secure before the loan officer today? but, how will I stand at all before God in eternity? One author put it this way:

> After all, life is short and eternity is long. One day I will stand before God. I cannot escape this encounter. It will take place. How can I be made right in his eyes? Or to give it a biblical ring, "What must I do to be saved?" Answer: "Believe in the Lord Jesus Christ and you shall be saved" (Acts 16:30–31). Believe. We are "made right" not by living a moral life (it would never be moral enough), or by good works (they would never be good enough), or by religious deeds (they would never be pious enough), but by faith alone in Christ alone.[13]

Preaching is about being saved, and what being saved entails. Preaching is about receiving the kingdom of God. In answer to the question, how is a person saved? preaching declares, "She is saved by faith in Christ." In addressing, how does a person receive the kingdom of God? preaching asserts, "She receives it by faith." And in answering, how does she know that the kingdom is near and can be received? preaching says, "She knows by the hearing of the preaching of faith; by the preaching of justification by faith alone." And to preach justification by faith alone is to preach that we *simul justus et peccator*—that we are both and at the same time "justified and sinner."

We are just and righteous in the sight of God not because of what we have done, but because of what Christ has done. We receive his perfection through faith and nothing else. We don't cooperate with his work on the cross. We don't supplement his work on the cross. We simply trust in his work as satisfying God's requirement of sinless perfection and righteousness on our behalf. And yet, we remain in the sinfulness of our flesh, daily battling to overcome temptation and often failing to do so. And yet our lack of faithfulness does not nullify the work of Christ on our behalf, because when we are faithless, he remains faithful (2 Tim. 2:13). In other words, our justification before God is not due to our righteousness; our righteousness is due to our justification before God in Christ.

The essence of *sola fide* is the answer to the age-old and all-important question, how is a sinful person accepted by a holy God? The *Heidelberg Catechism* asks and answers this question well:

Question 60: How art thou righteous before God?

Answer: Only by true faith in Jesus Christ; that is, although my conscience accuse me that I have grievously sinned against all the commandments of God, and have never kept any of them, and that I am still prone always to all evil, yet God, without any merit of mine, and of mere grace, grants and imputes to me the perfect satisfaction, righteousness, and holiness of Christ, as if I had never committed nor had any sin, and had myself accomplished all the obedience which Christ has fulfilled for me, if only I accept such benefit with a believing heart.

The egregious error of much of popular, modern preaching is that justification by faith has been replaced by eternally-damning notions of justification by wealth (God's pleasure is measured in one's money), justification by positive thinking (God's favor is on all, we just have to think positively about ourselves and God), justification by self-esteem (God's favor would be upon me if I would just see that I am worthy of it), and justification by death (God's favor is upon all who are funeralized in the church). All of these are popular impostors of the God-honoring, Christ-exalting, eternity-securing, and church-of-Christ-building justification by faith alone in Christ alone.[14]

If I could say anything to preachers today I would say, "Preach faith in Christ." Don't preach faith in Christ so that people might be rich—that is an abomination. Don't preach faith in Christ so that people might feel better about themselves—that is an aberration. Don't preach faith in Christ so that people might know how to win friends and influence people—that is degradation. Rather, preach faith in Christ so that people might know to live and die unto him. Preach faith in Christ so that people might understand and embrace the call to suffer loss for his name (Phil. 3:8). Preach faith in Christ so that people might know the riches of having sins forgiven, guilt removed, and eternity with Christ secured. Preach faith in Christ for God's glory and God's glory alone. John Piper has summed up the need and the call to preach *sola fide* in these words:

> Preaching and living justification by faith alone glorifies Christ, rescues hopeless sinners, emboldens imperfect saints, and strengthens fragile churches. It is a stunning truth—that God *justifies the ungodly by faith.* "To the one who does not work but trusts him who justifies the ungodly, his faith is counted as righteousness" (Rom. 4:5). History bears witness: the preaching of this truth creates, reforms, and revives the church.[15]

This is the message of the kingdom. This is the message that we must preach. It is the message of faith. Biblical preaching is preaching faith alone in Christ alone. If we could recover this and put aside the antics and the posturing, the fluff and the fantasy of the modern pulpit in general and the African-American pulpit in particular, we might see a Christianity that really changes people and changes our world. Our churches need changing. Preaching "faith alone" is one of the surest ways of facilitating that change.

When twentieth-century theologian J. Gresham Machen was dying, he telegraphed his friend and colleague, John Murray, with the words, "I am so glad for the active obedience of Christ. No hope without it." In reflecting upon these words of Machen, pastor Terry Johnson wrote:

> For years I was puzzled by these last words of Machen. Perhaps others have been puzzled as well. Now we are in a position to understand him. Machen was thinking of the righteousness of the perfect life of Christ that was imputed to him through faith. As death approached he found comfort and hope in Christ's atoning death through which his sins were pardoned (that is, through Christ's passive obedience). But especially precious to him at that moment was the knowledge of Christ's "active obedience", Christ's righteousness which was imputed to Machen. In the end, our theological details are not impractical abstractions. Rather, they provide the foundation for peace and joy even in the valley of the shadow of death, knowing that we shall stand before God, not naked, but clothed in the righteousness of Christ.[16]

Sola Gratia: The Light of the Gospel

The fourth of the *solas* is *sola gratia* or "grace alone." Grace alone means that it is by God's grace alone that we have been rescued from the wrath of God. His mercy and love toward us is not a response to our coming to him, but rather is the manifestation of his grace toward the elect.

Coming on the heels of faith alone, it would be easy (and indeed has been easy) to understand the act of believing, the exercising of faith in salvation, as meriting God's favor. In this sense faith could easily be seen as a work of righteousness whereby God is pleased to save because of what we have done. But the Bible makes it clear that though we exercise our faith unto salvation, our faith is not our own; God has graciously granted it to all those who believe (Phil. 1:29). We are also reminded plainly that faith is a gift from God, otherwise we might boast in its effectiveness (Eph. 2:8). "Grace alone" is a simple but necessary reminder that salvation that is by faith is a result of God's grace.

No preacher of the New Testament Scriptures should miss this. Why is it imperative that we be grace preachers, indeed, sovereign grace preachers? It is because all we are and all we have in God is by grace. Thus the faithful preacher is always calling his people to embrace the awesome grace of God.

We are saved by grace. There is nothing in our salvation experience that says, "Hey God, look at me." Rather, every time we reflect upon the goodness of Christ we are brought to the first principle—we are saved by grace. The preacher who preaches *sola gratia* reminds the people that they have not always been in the beloved of God. He reminds them that their now being in the beloved is not a result of who they are or what they have done. Grace is God's goodness despite our badness:

> For by grace you have been saved through faith. And this is not your own doing; it is the gift of God, not a result of works, so that no one may boast (Eph. 2:8–9).

> Who saved us and called us to a holy calling, not because of our works but because of his own purpose and grace, which he gave us in Christ Jesus before the ages began (2 Tim. 1:9).

We are sealed by grace. The grace that saves us is the grace that secures us. To preach grace is not only to preach that grace saves, but it is also to proclaim that it secures all those whom Christ saves. To preach that Christ saves a person, but that Christ does not secure him, is to preach another Christ and to not preach grace at all:

> And I am sure of this, that he who began a good work in you will bring it to completion at the day of Jesus Christ (Phil. 1:6).

> Blessed be the God and Father of our Lord Jesus Christ! According to his great mercy, he has caused us to be born again to a living hope

through the resurrection of Jesus Christ from the dead, to an inheritance that is imperishable, undefiled, and unfading, kept in heaven for you, who by God's power are being guarded through faith for a salvation ready to be revealed in the last time (1 Pet. 1:3–5).

We are sanctified by grace. Good preaching is often just a matter of asking and answering the right questions. When it comes to preaching grace, many of the important questions are questions of sanctification. To preach to a people who are *saved* by grace is to constantly remind them that they *live* by the grace of God as well. And so, the preacher is constantly asking: Has this world not overtaken you? Have you had any victories over the world or the flesh? Has the enemy been put to flight in any area of your life? Are you walking in the light of God's glory and goodness this year more than you were last year? Are you finding happiness and joy despite pain and sorrow? If the answer to any of these questions is yes, then take no credit unto yourself. It is grace. It is God's grace that not only saves but also sanctifies:

> For the grace of God has appeared, bringing salvation for all people, training us to renounce ungodliness and worldly passions, and to live self-controlled, upright, and godly lives in the present age (Titus 2:11–12).

We are satisfied by grace. Preaching that truly focuses upon the amazing grace of God and all that it means to God's people will produce in the people a hunger and a thirst for grace. This thirst and hunger will actually be a desire for God. Those so touched and amazed by the grace of God know of no greater pleasure and happiness than to live upon that grace. It is their only drink in a dry and weary land. The calling of the preacher is to create a thirst in the people and then to let them know that what they long for is God himself. God is the everlasting, all-satisfying, all-pleasing fount of joy. In our sermons our people should not only hear and sense that God saves and secures and sanctifies, but that he also amazingly satisfies. In the midst of everything else, his grace is the all-sufficient element:

But he said to me, "My grace is sufficient for you, for my power is made perfect in weakness." Therefore I will boast all the more gladly of my weaknesses, so that the power of Christ may rest upon me (2 Cor. 12:9).

We belittle grace and deny our people the best when we offer them financial security, self-esteem, positive-thinking, and even family values instead of the all-satisfying grace of God. Money will not satisfy when the doctors want to pull the plug on the life-support systems. People need grace. Positive thinking will not satisfy when a child drops out of school to join a cult. People need grace. Family values won't satisfy when she files divorce papers because she wants no part of the faith. People need grace. When Paul was suffering, God did not tell him that he needed to sow a seed. God did not tell him that he needed to look at the positive side of things. God did not tell him that he needed to give more attention to family values. He told Paul that Paul needed grace. Preacher, what are you telling your people? It's about grace, because it's about God. Preach grace, and grace alone! God will be glorified and your people will be glad.

Soli Deo Gloria: The Light of Glory
The last of the five *solas* is a fitting and glorious culmination of the first four. *Soli Deo gloria* means "to God alone the glory." Another way of stating this is to say that all glory belongs to God and God alone. This is the summation of the Christian life and the purpose for the existence of all things and beings. The Reformers, wanting to summate the life and doctrines of the Bible, declared in a phrase that all must find its life and purpose in God and God alone.

Here is where our modern preaching could use the most crucial facelift. Too frequently our pulpits are filled with men and women whose primary aim is to please.

Preaching for the glory of God is preaching that sees God's glory in all that God is doing and communicating to the world and his people. God's glory is in his creation. God's glory is in his character. God's glory is in his Christ.

God is jealous for his glory. We are reminded of this in Isaiah, where God says, "I am the LORD; that is my name; my glory I give to no other, nor my praise to carved idols" (Isa. 42:8). Also, God declares: "Everyone who is called by my name, whom I created for my glory, whom I formed and made" (Isa. 43:7). And again God says, "For my own sake, for my own sake, I do it, for how should my name be profaned? My glory I will not give to another" (Isa. 48:11).

"In our proud love affair with ourselves we pour contempt, whether we know it or not, upon the worth of God's glory."[17] A most appropriate goal of preaching is calling men and women to fall out of love with the world and themselves and to subsequently see the worth of falling in love with God. It is the task of proclaiming and demonstrating that there is unsurpassed gladness in magnifying the glory of God. Piper sums up what is preaching *soli Deo gloria* when he writes:

> My burden is to plead for the supremacy of God in preaching—that the dominant note of preaching be the freedom of God's sovereign grace, the unifying theme be the zeal that God has for his own glory, the grand object of preaching be the infinite and inexhaustible being of God, and the pervasive atmosphere of preaching be the holiness of God.[18]

What do I want from a sermon? I want the people to whom I preach to experience the truth. I don't want them just to hear the truth. I am not even satisfied if they understand the truth. My goal is that they would *experience* the truth. My goal is that they would experience him who is truth, namely Jesus Christ. Jesus Christ is real just as the truth is real. And if we are going to be faithful proclaimers of the truth, then we need to be preachers who lead people into the experience of Jesus Christ and the glories of his kingdom. Biblical preaching is calling people to an experience with the Word of God. Therefore biblical preaching is calling people to an experience with Jesus Christ, who is the Word made flesh and who is dwelling with us in grace and truth. (See appendix 1 for an example of how I prepare a sermon and appendix 2 for a sample sermon outline.)

May our preaching be a weekly demonstration of our commitments to this uncompromising reality. May God be glorified by our preaching, and may our people be glad he is.

4

BIBLICAL WORSHIP
Experiencing the Presence of God

by ANTHONY J. CARTER

The presence of the Lord is here
The presence of the Lord is here
I feel it in the atmosphere
The presence of the Lord is here. . . .

I can feel the presence of the Lord,
And I'm gonna get my blessing right now. . . .
                                    —Byron Cage

One of the more popular gospel songs in recent years has been a song announcing the presence of the Lord. The reason why the songwriter, and subsequent singers, can confidently say that the Lord is present is because he "feels" him. In fact, all can feel God's presence because it's like moisture; it's in the atmosphere. Therefore, *the presence of the Lord is here*. But what does the presence of the Lord mean? According to the song, it means that since I can feel the presence of the Lord, I am going to get my blessing. Right now! So the end of worship and the end of having the presence of God is to receive my blessing. *My* blessing suggests that it is the blessing I want. If we are honest, what the song is saying is that the present Lord is going to give me what I want, right now, because I demand it.

This song, as many songs, sums up what many people think of as "worship" today. The churches that likely sing this song demonstrate what worship has degenerated to in our time. Worship is nothing more than an event to serve my ends of getting what I want. It is the event in which the most powerful and extravagant genie ever discovered is let out of his bottle, and everyone present gets a free wish. This is the unfortunate state of worship in too many places that are known as churches in our land. Yet this is a far cry from worship as it is designed by God and delineated in the Scriptures.

What Is Worship?

Defining worship is not as easy as we might think. Worship is the life of the church. It is what we do. Yet sadly, few know what it is. Many can *describe* it, but rarely can they *define* it. I like to think of it in the same terms of trying to define "mother." Everyone has an idea of what "mother" means, yet when asked, individuals come up with their own nuanced, self-experienced definitions. So it is with "worship."

Nevertheless, numerous books have been written on the subject of worship. Each of these capable authors has defined the term ably, yet with a slightly distinct though not altogether different emphasis. John Frame, for example, states, "Worship is the work of acknowledging the greatness of our covenant Lord."[1] Wayne Grudem says, "Worship is the activity of glorifying God in His presence with our voices and hearts."[2] According to Ligon Duncan, worship is giving unto the Lord the glory due his name.[3] Louie Giglio gives perhaps the most insightful definition when he writes, "Worship is simply about value. The simplest definition I can give is this: Worship is our response to what we value most."[4] All of these definitions are accurate. They all point to the irrepressible truth that God and God alone is the one to whom worship is directed and for whom worship is designed. Nevertheless, for the sake of this chapter and in an attempt to contextualize my own experiences, I will piggyback on these definitions and define worship as *the activity and work of making much of God.*

Worship is making much of God. It is singing words that say he is great and I am not. It is speaking of his exaltation and my humiliation. It is praying for his perfect will and my patient acceptance. It is making much of him, whereby he is seen as increasing in esteem and I as decreasing (John 3:30). To this end worship is not only a once- or twice-a-week activity. Making much of God is not simply what I do on Sunday morning or evening or Wednesday evening. On the contrary, it becomes the warp and woof of the Christian life.

The first question raised in the *Westminster Shorter Catechism* is, "What is the chief end of man?" In other words, what is the primary goal for which humanity was created? The primary goal, according to the *Shorter Catechism*, is "to glorify God, and to enjoy him forever." To glorify God, is to worship him. How important is worship? It is the end, the goal, the purpose of all living. Rick Warren, the author of the popular book *The Purpose-Driven Life*, describes the purpose-driven life as the worshipful life: a life that reflects the first question of the catechism.[5]

The Bible describes worship as *service.* To worship God, according to the Scriptures, is to serve God. The Old Testament illustrates this when God called Moses to lead the children of Israel out of Egypt. After God spoke to Moses at the burning bush on Mount Horeb, the mountain of God, Moses expressed his apprehension about going to Pharaoh. He asked God, "Who am I that I should go to Pharaoh and bring the children of Israel out of Egypt?" (Ex. 3:11). God responded to Moses by letting him know, "I will be with you, and this shall be the sign for you, that I have sent you: when you have brought the people out of Egypt, you shall *serve* God on this mountain" (Ex. 3:12). When God gave the word to Moses to lead Israel out of Egypt, the end of their deliverance was not the deliverance itself, but *service*; indeed, it was worship. In the original language of the text, the word for *service* is *abad*. *Abad* means "to work, to serve," and it carries the connotation of *worship*. The New American Standard Version of the Bible, as well as others, translates the end of verse 12 as, "you shall *worship* God at this mountain."[6] God called Israel out of Egypt not simply to relieve them from the yoke of slavery, but more importantly that they might enjoy that for which they were created, the worship of God. And who is the God they were called to worship? He is the eternal, covenant-establishing, covenant-keeping God, who called a people who were not a people and declared that those who worship him shall be his people and he their God (Ex. 6:7). In the New Testament the goal is the same.

As a response to the depths of the glories and riches of God in salvation, Paul appeals to us "to present our bodies as a living sacrifice, holy and acceptable to God, which is our spiritual *worship*" (Rom. 12:1). The word translated *worship* in the original Greek language is the word *latriea*. *Latriea* means "service, divine worship." The King James Version translates the end of verse 1 as, "which is your reasonable service." It is the word from which we derive the English word *liturgy*. Consequently, we see in the New Testament, just as we saw in the Old Testament, that worship is service. It is rendering unto God the reasonable and proper response to his setting us free from the bondage of sin. It is our response to him whom we value more than anything else. According to two authors, "Service is the work and duty of a servant to and for a superior and good service is that which pleases the superior."[7] In this sense, when we refer to our gathering times as "worship services," we are actually speaking redundantly, though accurately. How appropriate is it that our weekly gatherings should begin with a call to worship—a call to service.

Since the Bible reminds us that worship is service, we may lament the popular trend of replacing the expression "worship service" with the more palatable phrases "worship celebration" or "worship experience." These phrases, while seeking to capture the existential and uplifting aspects of worship, threaten to undermine the fundamental biblical principle of worship, which is service.[8]

In spite of the clear teaching in the Scriptures that worship is service to God, Christians in too many of our churches today are far more interested in being served rather than serving. When they go to church, they are more interested in what they get than what they give. They are more concerned with being entertained than being edified. Subsequently, the sad state of affairs is that more often than not entertainment has replaced worship. Yet we need to understand that worship is not entertainment.

What Worship Is Not

The historical predominantly black church has found itself often at the crossroads of worship and entertainment. It has practically become folklore for those in the black music industry who find success to have gotten their start in the church. From Aretha Franklin to Whitney Houston, from Sam Cook to R. Kelly, most of the African-American music elite are fond of referring to their roots in the church as being the catalyst for their careers. While this sounds noble and even admirable, something about this scenario should cause us to pause and reflect upon the life of the church.

In the 1930s as gospel music was growing among predominantly black churches in America, the gospel superstar began to emerge. Along with the emergence of this new personality phenomenon came the inevitable temptation to begin mixing the success of gospel music in church with the potential money-making venture of taking that talent to the streets. More and more, men and women who found success in singing to and wooing the church found it lucrative to take their voices to the popular culture. The first to find broad success and set the game for others to follow was the renowned gospel diva Rosetta Tharpe.

Born in 1915 Arkansas and raised under the influence of her Holiness evangelist mother, Rosetta Tharpe found a quick place for her prodigious musical abilities. Skillfully playing the guitar before age six, she would grow to transcend the traditions of her Holiness upbringing and find unparalleled recognition and success. According to one historian:

America had never seen—nor has it seen since—anyone quite like Rosetta Tharpe. She was the Madonna of her day—fearlessly challenging roles and costumes and social mores. She was Dolly Parton of her day—irrepressible, unfazed by criticism, a sexy girl from the country. She was Queen Latifah of her day—larger than life, lavishly talented, able to move between seemingly irreconcilable worlds with consummate ease. "Before Tharpe," notes Jerma A. Jackson, "gospel singers enjoyed mostly local reputations in the African American communities in which they were a part. Performing in New York nightclubs and theaters, Tharpe extended the music to new audiences: secular, middle-class, and white."[9]

Tharpe's crossover appeal was chronicled in the April 28, 1939, issue of *Life* magazine in an article entitled, "Singer Swings Same Songs in Church and Night Club."[10] A description of the article reads:

> The top picture features Tharpe performing with a large orchestra at the Church of God in Christ in Harlem. The bottom picture shows Tharpe dressed in white singing at the Cotton Club in Harlem, surrounded by jitterbugging dancers.[11]

Following Tharpe's lead has been a plethora of unfortunate, successful, and tragic lives of men and women who first found success in the church only to be lured by the profits of the world.[12] But we must ask, what has been the result of this incessant desire to take the church's talent to the popular world? Has the church been better for it? Have those who have endeavored to find that illusive balance between the church and world actually found it and become faithful disciples and representatives of Christ? The answer to these questions is an emphatic, no! And yet we continue to see this phenomenon and even laud it. The predominantly African-American church is impressed with the star personality to such a degree that flitting between the altar and the auditorium, the sacred praise and secular applause, is so common that one can hardly tell the difference. Worship in such churches is no more about biblical worship than the popular movie *Gospel* was about the gospel.

Looking at the landscape of the predominantly African-American church should make us examine our idea of worship. Maybe we should ask, why is it so easy to move from the sacred altar to the secular auditoriums and vice versa? I would suggest that the reason so many musical performers can move so comfortably in and out of the church is because the lines between worship and entertainment have been blurred.

Biblical worship is not a sanctified worldly event. In other words, it is not taking the methods and means the world employs to produce a good time and using them to produce a "good time in the Lord." That may be sanctified entertainment, but that is not worship. Worship is other-worldly. It is an encounter with Jesus that takes us out of this world. It is so distinct that those who are most in tune with the world will know unmistakably that the event on Sunday morning or even Saturday evening is something distinct and different—appropriately causing them to draw back in fear or draw near in awe.

Worship is not entertainment. There is a thin line between worship and entertainment, particularly among African-Americans. Nevertheless, it is a line that must be drawn and maintained if we are ever going to know and teach what it means to worship well. Though there may be some entertaining qualities to worship, and those who are enthralled by the entertainment industry do exhibit characteristics of worship,[13] nevertheless, worship and entertainment have two differing and conflicting agendas. Entertainment is predominantly passive, whereas worship is predominantly active. Entertainment is audience-driven. Worship is God-driven. We must understand this if we are going to worship well.

Unfortunately, we often want worship to be entertainment because this is what we get during the week. And we might not even realize it. You see, from television to the theater, from computer programs to computer games, from instant messaging to instant coffee, this generation is treated to a wealth of entertainment, information, and resources graphically designed and instantly delivered. Life is fast-paced. It is always new and improved. This creates a low threshold for the slow-paced, meditative, reflective life that is often

Christianity. The result is an easy boredom and a lack of appreciation for the quietness and stillness that hearing from God often requires. Thus when we come to church, we want what we so readily receive all week long—fast-paced, up-to-the-minute, quality, graphic entertainment. Unfortunately, too many places on Sunday morning are eager to give people what they want in an effort to reach them, or more accurately, to woo them into membership. When this happens, according to Marva Dawn, "the focus then becomes not so much to display the glory of God as to delight the people who come."[14] What we don't realize is that these places are doing nothing more than scratching a worldly people where they itch. They are perpetuating a superficial faith. They never penetrate to the deeper places of humanity and substantial Christian experience. This superficiality fails to lead people to see that a lasting relationship with God is not accomplished in a fast-paced, hurried, entertainment-driven mode. It comes by getting before God and spending time, often long and quiet times, with him. This indispensable exercise of Christian devotion is what church is supposed to prepare people for. This is what the church is to prepare people to encounter—a God who is bigger and better than we first imagined, but is never boring, even in the quietest times. This should be a goal of our worship.

The world in which we live is personality driven. We are fascinated by the most flamboyant, outgoing, media savvy personalities. Whether it is the flamboyancy of sports stars like Dennis Rodman, the captivating looks and personality of movie star Halle Berry, or the media and political savvy of former president Bill Clinton, we are mesmerized by big, larger-than-life personalities. We find them entertaining, even captivating, though we may or may not like their views or lifestyles. We find it hard not to pay attention, and we want to know where they are and what they say. Unfortunately, too often this is what we want in our worship as well.

The most exciting, well attended predominantly black churches in America tend to be those that seek to appeal to our depraved culture and our tendency to delight in our expressions of depravity. This depravity is manifested in our desire to be entertained and our narcissistic drive for everything self. According to George Barna and Harry Jackson in *High Impact African-American Churches*:

> The atmosphere of celebration at high-impact black churches appeals to many young adults who have been raised in a culture that is saturated with entertainment, marketing, and hedonism. . . . High impact black churches, in particular, connect with many young adults through the animated practical preaching style that makes corporate worship a more passionate and inviting endeavor.[15]

Barna and Jackson have rightly diagnosed the state of these churches, yet they go on to commend this philosophy of "entertainment, marketing and hedonism" in worship. Rather than commend this worldly approach to worship, we should lament that such is being pawned off as worship today. We do not gather on Sunday morning to delight worldly-minded sinners, but rather we gather to delight in the wonders of God. Yet can our worldly minds be entertained, can we make mass appeal to our sinful hedonism, and simultaneously delight and magnify the greatness of God? The answer is emphatically, no! When we cross over into the worship of God, there should be a marked difference between what the world enjoyed on Saturday night and what the saints offer on Sunday morning.

Whereas the world is personality driven, worship should be Christ-driven. Yet far too often what is passed off as worship today is nothing more than the Sunday morning, sanitized version of personality worship. We have so bought into the notion of being fascinated with people that when we come to worship on Sunday there is little to excite us except that which makes the people we admire most seem larger than life. In this sense we should lament that Christianity today has become personality driven. The popularity of the flamboyant Juanita Bynum-Weeks should not surprise us. The popularity of the attention-hawking Eddie Long should not surprise us. The popularity of the media and marketing savvy T. D. Jakes should not surprise us. The consequence of this downward spiral is that there is more showmanship in preaching than there is substance. This is the state of our culture. This also, regretfully, is the state of the church.

What Happens in Worship

How do we overcome the influence of the world and not have our Christianity and our worship overtaken by personalities and people? First, we need to stop being so entertainment or personality driven in our day-to-day lives. As Christians, we should realize how much of an influence our day-to-day living has on our worship. If we are taken in with *Ebony* and *Essence* magazines, if soap operas and sporting events give us emotional and relational highs, if Oprah Winfrey and Tom Joyner provide us with philosophical substance for living, then we have little hope of being truly Christ-centered on Sunday morning. As we seek to fulfill the calling to have our minds renewed and not be conformed to this world's ways (Rom. 12:1–2), we will find that worship that is appropriate for redeemed creatures to offer is worship that is unspotted by the world's fascination with personalities.

Second, we must know what the Bible says happens in worship. Congregations coming together on Sunday morning or Wednesday evening are not just a collection of warm bodies who desire to be friendly to one another because of a like confession of faith. Rather, there are important and indispensable spiritual realities that take place. If we were more aware of these spiritual realities, how we prepare for worship and how we engage in worship would be transformed.

We Meet with God

The first spiritual reality is that we meet with God (Heb. 12:22–29):

> But you have come to Mount Zion and to the city of the living God, the heavenly Jerusalem, and to innumerable angels in festal gathering, and to the assembly of the firstborn who are enrolled in heaven, and to God, the judge of all, and to the spirits of the righteous made perfect, and to Jesus, the mediator of a new cov-

enant, and to the sprinkled blood that speaks a better word than the blood of Abel.

See that you do not refuse him who is speaking. For if they did not escape when they refused him who warned them on earth, much less will we escape if we reject him who warns from heaven. At that time his voice shook the earth, but now he has promised, "*Yet once more* I will shake not only the earth but also the heavens." This phrase, "Yet once more," indicates the removal of things that are shaken—that is, things that have been made—in order that the things that cannot be shaken may remain. Therefore let us be grateful for receiving a kingdom that cannot be shaken, and thus let us offer to God acceptable worship, with reverence and awe, for our God is a consuming fire.

Meeting with God is no cavalier occurrence. It is an awe-inspiring and soul-shaking event. Isaiah gives us an intimate glimpse into our meeting with God. According to Isaiah 6:1–6, when we meet with God we are reminded that God is holy, untouched or spotted by sin or unrighteousness. He is great, without equal or peer in all heaven and earth. He is accustomed to being worshipped continually. The angelic beings are in continuous, antiphonal, harmonious praise of his thrice holiness. He is heavy; his glory fills the entirety of the heavenly temple, and all those in attendance experience the weightiness of his presence, particularly those humans who have been called.

When Isaiah is brought into the worshipful presence of God, he is overwhelmed by God's glory and weight. God's powerful holiness overwhelms Isaiah, and he is fearful for his life, because he is sinful in his nature. The holiness of God reveals more plainly and undeniably the sinfulness of humans. Isaiah came to understand this and cried out, "Woe is me! For I am lost; for I am a man of unclean lips, and I dwell in the midst of a people of unclean lips . . ." (Isa. 6:5). Isaiah gets a clear picture of himself because he has been given a clear picture of his God. John Calvin described this overwhelming phenomenon that Isaiah experienced when he wrote, "It is evident that man never attains to a true self-knowledge until he have previously contemplated the face of God, and come down after such contemplation to look into himself."[16] When we come into worship, we should come expecting to meet with God, but this meeting with God should cause us to see ourselves more clearly. We should get a right and real understanding of our unworthiness and God's eternal, incalculable value. If we ever grasped the reality that God has called us to meet with him in worship, it would change not only how we approach worship, but what we do in worship.

We Fellowship with Christ

The second spiritual reality in worship is that we fellowship with Christ (Heb. 2:10–13):

> For it was fitting that he, for whom and by whom all things exist, in bringing many sons to glory, should make the founder of their salvation perfect through suffering. For he who sanctifies and those who are sanctified all have one source. That is why he is not ashamed to call them brothers, saying,
>
> > "I will tell of your name to my brothers;
> > in the midst of the congregation I will sing your praise."
>
> And again,
>
> > "I will put my trust in him."
>
> And again,
>
> > "Behold, I and the children God has given me."

One of the amazing realities of worship is that we do not worship God by ourselves. Indeed, it would be presumptuous for us to believe that with these sinful hands and from these iniquity-laden hearts we could offer anything of value and worth to the service and worship of God. On the contrary, the only acceptable offering we make to God is the offering we make in Christ Jesus our Lord. In Christ we have not only the forgiveness of sin (Eph. 1:7; Col. 1:14) but also access to the throne of God, where we can go boldly with our praise (Heb. 4:14–16). And the writer of Hebrews reminds us that we do not go alone. Christ goes with us and gladly and joyfully joins in the singing of praises to God. Would it not make us more diligent in the selection of songs if we were more aware that Christ wants to stand next to us and share our hymnal?

We Encourage One Another

The third spiritual reality is that we encourage one another in worship (Heb. 10:24–25):

> And let us consider how to stir up one another to love and good works, *not neglecting to meet together, as is the habit of some, but encouraging one another,* and all the more as you see the Day drawing near.

People today are fond of asking whether someone can be a Christian if he or she does not go to church. The New Testament is too full of "one another" passages for people to believe that they can live faithfully and pleasingly before God in isolation from other believers.[17] God has created the church as a body, a living organism. One part of the body cannot simply decide to stop functioning or to function on its own and expect the church to remain healthy. The church is designed to be a "one another" institution.

When we gather for worship, one of the important realities is that we testify to our being there for one another. We exhort one another. We edify one another. We challenge one another. We admonish one another. We pray for and with one another. We share with one another our time, our treasures, and our talents. We teach one another. And we equip one another. Therefore, I must be reminded that I do not go to church for myself. I go to church for all those who have come to church for me. The most selfish act a Christian can do is stay away from the gathered body of Christians. To stay away is to deny my brothers and sisters the fellowship and encouragement only I can give. God has designed the church in such a marvelous way as to have us intricately interdependent upon each other for his glory. This is a reality that takes place whether we realize it or not.

Scripture powerfully reminds us that worship is not a casual, take-it-or-leave-it proposition. On the contrary, God is serious about and jealous for his worship. Christ is present and even expects to join in the praises of God. And we are never to believe that worship is something we can do at home alone;it is designed for the communion of the saints. Once we begin contemplating these realities, we will inevitably think more soberly about what we so flippantly call worship today. We will seek to design our worship service according to a desire to reflect the "reverence and awe" God so rightly deserves. We will worship well.

How to Worship Well

The first step in worshiping well is to realize that we are worship beings. We were created to worship, and evidence of this truth is all around us. Whenever humans have discovered other humans, those humans were found worshiping. From the deep recesses of uncharted rainforest to the plush high-rises of New York City, humans are paying homage to someone or something. It is an innate response. It is the manifestation of what theologians refer to as the *sensus divinitatis,* the innate sense of the divine that we are created to express. And though sin has caused the creature to pervert this gift and to worship creation rather than the Creator (Rom. 1:25), the redeemed in this world have been reconstituted to fulfill our primary purpose—to worship and adore God. Interestingly, by commanding us to love him with all our heart, mind, and strength (Deut. 6:5), God is commanding us to worship him with all aspects of our created being: *emotional, physical, and intellectual.*

Christians are called to be, at some level, intellectual beings; we are commanded to use our minds in the pursuit of God. We are commanded to develop a Christian worldview that is mind-renewing (Rom. 12:2). We are called to have a mind that is brought into conformity to the mind of Christ (Phil. 2:5), where every thought is brought captive to the obedience of Christ (2 Cor. 10:5). Scripture presumes that we are intellectual beings. Undeniably, God has chosen to communicate to us through the written and preached word, thereby engaging our mental, intellectual capabilities. In theological circles, the "primacy of the intellect" is the view that truth comes to a person first through the intellect and only subsequently is applied to the will and emotions. And yet, affirming that the Word of God primarily is to be heard and/or read, we also realize that we are not simply intellectual beings. As John Frame reminds us:

> Certainly, God made the intellect to inform our actions and feelings, and there are grave dangers in living by one's feelings apart from intellectual reflection. But in Scripture, God addresses his word, not to "the intellect" but to the whole person, to the "heart." It is the whole person who has fallen into sin and must be redeemed.[18]

Subsequently, we also are to worship God with our emotional self.

The worship of God with our emotions is controversial in many theological circles. Many see the misapplication of Scripture and the erratic behavioral worship patterns of some charismatic groups and conclude that an emphasis upon feelings and emotions inevitably leads to unbiblical and irreverent worship. Though I agree that Scripture does not justify barking like a dog and convulsing on the floor and that there is nothing reverent about emotional orgies, we must not let these excesses, due to an over-emphasis upon feelings and emotions, deny us the right, God-glorifying place of feelings and emotions in the worship of our God. Contrary to popular mischaracterizations, Reformed theology has long seen the important place of emotions in God's dealing with and speaking to his people, and therefore has seen scripturally that emotions are indispensable in the worship of our God.[19]

Scripture prominently mentions several emotions, and they should play a role in our worship. First, no one can deny that joy is scripturally relevant to those who worship. The psalmist declared, "Make a joyful noise to the LORD, all the earth; break forth into joyous song and sing praises" (Ps. 98:4). Joy is an emotion that is expressed through our voices with shouts and singing. It is expressed through our instruments in melodious tones.

Second, Scripture reminds us of our need to express sorrow, particularly sorrow for our sin. Again the psalmist demonstrates that we need to reflect upon our need for forgiveness and that the sacrifices that please God are "a broken spirit; a broken and contrite heart" (Ps. 51:17). Sorrow and joy are emotions that mature Christians understand go together and are often expressed in similar form. Tears of sorrow should inevitably give way to tears of joy. In other words, "Weeping may tarry for the night, but joy comes with the morning" (Ps. 30:5).

Third, there should be the experience of reverence and awe. The writer of Hebrews tells us that acceptable worship to God is worship that is accompanied with reverence and awe (Heb. 12:28). Reverence is simply a deep respect and affection. In other words, it is the demonstration of an affection that is tempered with respect for the one being revered. If anything needs to be reiterated in the predominantly African-American church today it is the biblical mandate that the worship of God must be tempered with a respect for God. It is not that God does not expect and even desire our emotional expressions of love and adoration. Of course he does. What loving father would not want the love and adoration of his children? However, that display of affection must always be tempered with a respect that determines the means and the extent of that display. Unrestrained emotional outbursts in the name of adoring God are not biblical worship. Unrestrained affections are representative of irreverent orgies, not worship.

Awe is defined as fear mingled with reverence and inspiration. The fear of God has been lost in too many predominantly African-American church services. To fear God is to know God. To not fear him is to not know him. To fear God is to understand that the God who gives us life is the God who takes our lives. It is to comprehend that the God who gives us our health is the God who takes our health from us. To fear God is to understand that the same God who raised Christ from the grave is the same God who sent him to the cross. Inspired worship is worship that sees God as sovereign. And an ultimate Sovereign is to be feared even while he is being adored.

Last, while many sincere Christians prefer to quietly sit still and worship God, the worship of God in Scripture is often accompanied by physical expressions. Frequently, the lifting of hands gave expression in prayer and praise to the idea of drawing near to God and the readiness to receive from him (Neh. 8:6; Pss. 28:2; 63:4). Worship of God with the feet of his saints is demonstrated by those who danced in praise of God (Ex. 15:20; 2 Sam. 6:14; Ps. 150:4).[20] And though many find it irreverent, Scripture reminds us that there is a place for the clapping of hands in our worship of God (Ps. 47:1).[21]

What to Do in Worship

How shall we worship? If we asked ten churchgoers this question, we might expect to receive ten different, even contradictory answers. This is due in part to a lack of knowledge concerning what the Bible actually says about worship. Many people think that although worship is a major theme of Scripture, the Bible does not tell so much "how" we are to worship but is most concerned with "who" we are to worship. Looking at the first four commandments (Ex. 20:2–11), Barna and Jackson have said:

> (God) did not tell the Israelites how to worship God so much as to exhort them to ensure that they engaged Him—and only Him—in worship. By providing the motivation but not the methods related to worship, the Lord left open the door for varied expressions of our hearts to Him, resulting in the widespread styles of worship encountered in churches and denominations around the world today.[22]

Such statements should cause us to wonder if God cares how we worship him at all. If Barna and Jackson are right, one form of worship is equally as valid as another form. Consequently, the God of truth has acquiesced to relativism and has left to the whims of sinful human beings the guidelines for the central function of the church—worship. This I do not accept. This we need not accept because the Bible does tell us much about the worship of God, both in terms of method and motive. John Frame makes this point when he writes:

> Therefore, we must seek above all to do what pleases [God]. To do this, we cannot trust our own imaginations. Nadab and Abihu trusted their own wisdom, and God judged them severely. Can any of us trust ourselves to determine, apart from Scripture, what God does and does not like in worship? Our finitude and sin disqualify us from making such judgments. For such a serious decision—potentially a life-and-death decision—we must seek God's own wisdom.[23]

In this book, we are commending the Reformed tradition because we are convinced that the Reformed Christian approach holds the most biblically accurate and historically consistent understanding of the Christian life. This also extends to the area of worship. Historically, the Reformed tradition has advocated what is known as the *regulative principle of worship*. According to the *Baptist Confession of Faith* (1689):

> The light of nature shows that there is a God, who has lordship and sovereignty over all; is just, good and does good to all; and is therefore to be feared, loved, praised, called upon, trusted in, and served, with all the heart and all the soul, and with all the might. But the acceptable way of worshiping the true God, is instituted by himself, and so limited by his own revealed will, that he may not be worshiped according to the imagination and devices of men, nor the suggestions of Satan, under any visible representations, or any other way not prescribed in the Holy Scriptures.[24]

In short, the regulative principle of worship says that our intentional aspects of our worship service toward him are to be only what God has prescribed in the Bible. We are not to worship him in a way inappropriate and inconsistent with his nature (see Deut. 12:4). Rather, we are to do what he commands and how he commands it (see Deut. 12:32). This is the consistent expression of the Reformation mantra *sola Scriptura*.

The Bible must serve as our guide in our worship. We are not to be taken in by the world's methods or motives. We are to examine every element of our worship service so as to find biblical warrant and justification for the use of that element in the worship of God. Melva Costen writes:

> *Use Scripture to undergird the entire worship event.* The use of a lectionary would be helpful, but is not required. Each of the elements in the order of worship should reflect an interweaving of the Scripture(s) and the sermon, so that the congregation might be led to a well-rounded worship experience.[25]

And yet, it is not enough just to examine the elements, but we must also actively set forth a worship that is consistent with our theology. The Bible has a high view of God, so too should our worship. The Bible has a clear and consistent analysis of the human condition, so our worship should reflect this truth. The Bible has an unmistakable emphasis on the person and work of Jesus Christ on our behalf, so too should our worship. The Bible consistently reminds us that we are to make less of ourselves and much of God, so too should our worship. This is the essence of biblically-deduced, God-exalting, human-humbling, and Christ-adoring worship.

The Bible is God's Word about God. It is the primary source for us knowing who God is and how God works. When we enter into worship, our goal should be to say about God what God says about God. Therefore the Bible is indispensable. Ligon Duncan suggests an excellent approach: "Read the Bible, preach the Bible, pray the Bible, sing the Bible, and see the Bible."[26] Unfortunately, in the majority of churches in America, particularly predominantly African-American churches, the Bible is nothing more than a prop or an institutional icon. It is present, but we rarely read it, we sporadically preach it, we hardly pray it, we sparingly sing it, and we reluctantly see it. Recovering biblical worship in our churches will begin with the recovery of the Bible as the guide for worship.

Read the Bible (1 Tim. 4:13; Luke 4:16–21). Reading the Bible in worship would seem to be a no-brainer. However, in recent times the public reading of Scripture has found less and less prominence in our churches. This is an unfortunate reality and may be indicative of our lack of understanding concerning the Bible's character. African-American Christians, according to statistics, are more likely to believe in the divine inspiration and inerrancy of the Bible than any demographic group.[27] And yet in many churches the Word of God is not intentionally read, apart from the jump-off point for the sermon. However, we must understand that of all the words that are spoken during the Sunday morning worship service, the only words of which we can be one 100 percent assured are true and unmingled with error are those words we read directly from the Bible. God unequivocally speaks to us when we read his Word. Therefore, we should seek to read the Bible at every opportunity.

Preach the Bible (Neh. 8:1–8; 2 Tim. 4:2). Preaching lays the foundation for the church. As Ligon Duncan so aptly states, "Preaching is God's prime appointed instrument to build up his church. As Paul says, 'faith comes from hearing' (see Rom. 10:14–17)."[28] In the historic African-American church, the preacher has long been regarded as the mouthpiece of God. As one historian has written:

> The time of preaching in worship enabled slaves to hear and experience the Word, good news of liberation, salvation and sanctification. This necessitated a person, divinely inspired, called by God, and affirmed by the community, who could stand in the divine place (at the improvised pulpit) and deliver the Word. Also required was some knowledge of the Bible, combined with the ability to speak and communicate this sacred knowledge. The preacher, therefore, played an important role as mediator/priest and especially prophet.[29]

The person of the preacher and the content of the Word preached have always been inseparable and indispensable in the life of the church.[30] And yet in our times, preaching has lost its centrality because of the emphasis on entertainment, music, and musicians. The unfortunate result has been too many preachers who have developed methods of preaching that more resemble the theater or

Broadway than Paul's admonition to Timothy: "Preach the word" (2 Tim. 4:2).

Paul did not tell Timothy to sing a song or recite a poem, but rather to "preach the word." So, what should we preach? We should preach the Word. Not ourselves, not our lofty, highly persuasive opinions, but rather the Word of God. We must insist that our preachers not engage in amateurish theatrics but rather deal plainly, clearly, and even creatively with the text of Scripture, and with the text alone. Again Duncan is right: "People who appreciate the Bible's teaching on worship will have a high view of preaching, and little time for the personality driven, theologically-void, superficially practical, monologues that pass for preaching today."[31]

Pray the Bible (Matt. 21:13; 1 Tim. 2:1). Prayer is the petitioning of God to faithfully do, for his glory and our good, what he has promised to do. But how will we know what he has promised to do unless we know what the Bible says? When we pray according to the will of God, we are praying according to the Word of God. God's house has always been called a house of prayer (Matt. 21:13) because it has always been a house of his Word. Therefore, if we would be the house of prayer that God calls us to be, we must be a house that prays according to his Word. Terry Johnson has made the case this way:

> The pulpit prayers of Reformed churches should be rich in biblical and theological content. Do we not learn the language of Christian devotion from the Bible? Do we not learn the language of confession and penitence from the Bible? Do we not learn the promises of God to believe and claim in prayer from the Bible? Don't we learn the will of God, the commands of God, and the desires of God for His people, for which we are to plead in prayer, from the Bible? Since these things are so, public prayers should repeat and echo the language of the Bible throughout.[32]

Sing the Bible (Ps. 98:1; Eph. 5:19). When most people think about worship, the primary expression that comes to mind is singing. The tradition of heartfelt, skillful, inspirational music in the African-American Christian experience goes way back. Even before black

Christians could read or write, they could sing the praises of God. In fact, singing in worship service was an intensified expression of singing in everyday life for the black slave in America. "One did not stop whatever else one was doing to sing."[33] From the early developments of the spirituals to the incorporation and improvisation of traditional hymns and from the introduction of Gospel music to the modern, contemporary Gospel scene, music has had an unequalled tradition and influence upon the life and direction of the black church in America. While singing in the black church has proved to be indispensable, too often it has proved to be determinant of what good worship is as well. As one author has written concerning singing in the African-American church context:

> It is possible to have church without outstanding preaching, but not without good singing. It can fill the vacuum of a poor sermon. Good singing is impassioned, intense, emotional, and spiritually powerful. This is due to the conviction about what sermon the soloists and choir are delivering in song.[34]

The unfortunate reality is that too often the sermon the soloist or choir is delivering is not biblical. This is because we have not adhered to the principle of singing the Bible. To sing the Bible simply means to make sure that our songs say about God what God has said about God. The words of our songs should be steeped in biblical content and references. While we sing songs that relate our experiences with God and his grace (e.g. "Amazing Grace," by John Newton), we must be diligent in assuring the theological accuracy of songs that are written today.

When singing the songs of artists such as Thomas Dorsey, James Cleveland, Trumaine Hawkins, and Kurt Franklin, the African-American church, while enjoying the fruits of skillful performers, has not been diligent in making sure the songs we sing are founded upon biblical and theological truths. And yet we understand that the worship of God is best where the gospel of God is truest.

It is not a matter of traditional versus contemporary; it is a matter of biblical versus unbiblical. Surely many of the hymns we sing have stood the tests of time and the Bible. And many contemporary songs will undoubtedly do the same. Yet let us not get slack in our insistence that these songs stand up to biblical scrutiny. This scrutiny needs to be even sharper in our day because biblical discernment is at an all-time low. A biblical and therefore worshipful contemporary song for your consideration is "Total Praise" by Richard Smallwood. Smallwood considers the opening words of Psalm 121 and puts to music, "Lord, I will lift my eyes to the hills." He ends his short, yet inspirational chorus with a reference to Psalm 63:4, "I lift my hands in total praise to You. Amen."[35] Another contemporary hymn that is getting much mileage in Reformed churches, and should get more in African-American churches, is the hymn "In Christ Alone" by Keith Getty and Stuart Townend. Getty and Townend build upon the reformational truth of *solus Christus*, Christ Alone, and remind us in verse that "in Christ Alone my hope is found. He is my light, my strength, my song; this cornerstone, this solid ground; firm through the fiercest drought and storm."[36]

There are some differences between these two songs. "In Christ Alone" is more in the form of traditional hymnody and would find little opposition to usefulness in a wide range of churches today. "Total Praise" is in the form of a modern chorus with an urban tone. It would find fewer acceptances in a variety of Christian expressions. The former is more theologically complex and thoughtful. The latter emphasizes the simplicity and devotional aspects of Christian expression. Which of the two is more useful and thus more worshipful? Admittedly, the usefulness of a song for worship is not determined by its contemporary or traditional composition. It is not determined by its simplicity or complexity. It may not even hinge on the instrument upon which it is played. Rather, we must ask, does the song invoke reverence and awe? Does it draw me close to God in humble submission? Ultimately, does it say about God what God says about God? Both of these songs answer these questions in the affirmative. Both of these songs reflect the biblical, theological, and experiential aspects of historical Christianity.

One sure way of making sure that our songs say about God what God has said about God is to spend more time singing the Psalms.

In the Psalms, God has given his people a wealth of poetic expressions of worship. If I could commend anything to the worship of the predominantly African-American church today it would be the deliberate incorporation of the Psalms into our repertoire of worship songs. I am not advocating exclusive psalm singing, as some in the Reformed tradition advocate. However, I am suggesting that the use of the Psalms would serve us well in not only assuring that the words we sing are acceptable to God, but also that the words would undoubtedly be encouraging and edifying to all who sing them.[37] When we worship God with the words of God's own mouth, we are more likely to offer him worship with reverence and awe, which is an acceptable and pleasing aroma.

Music in church is to serve the Word. In other words, it is to prepare the people to hear from God, while giving expression to their hearts before God.

See the Bible (1 Cor. 11:23–26; Rom. 6:3–4; Col. 2:11–12). While it may strike some as strange to speak about the notion of "seeing" the Bible in worship, actually visually observing the Word of God is an intriguing part of our worship of him. When we say "see the Bible," we are simply saying that there needs to be the regular observance of the sacraments—baptism and the Lord's Supper—in our worship services. In the Lord's Supper and baptism we behold the central elements of the drama of our redemption. We are given a visible demonstration of the gospel that we preach. In the bread of communion we see the body of Christ, which was given for us (Luke 22:19). In the wine of communion we see the blood of Christ, which was poured out for the forgiveness of our sins (Matt. 26:27). In baptism we see the cleansing power of regeneration and new life as we are unified with Christ in his death, burial, and resurrection (Rom. 6:3–4; 1 Pet. 3:21). These are the grandest dramas of redemption in the church. In fact, according to Duncan:

> The sacraments (baptism and the Lord's Supper) are the only two commanded dramas of Christian worship. . . . In them we see the promise of God. But we could also say that in the sacraments we see, smell, touch, and taste the word.[38]

Most African-American churches observe the Lord's Supper on a monthly basis and baptism as frequently as necessary. While I am not arguing for the frequency of these important elements of worship, I do believe that our worship services would be well served to consider these elements as not mere commemorations of an event, but also as the visible, dramatic display of God's present promises to his people in Christ. To know that we see the promises of God and not just hear them will undoubtedly change the way we view the sacraments and our worship of God as well.

How Will It Be

What will this worship look like in an African-American setting? Let me reiterate: the Bible must be our guide for how and what we do in our worship service. Therefore each element of worship should have a biblical mandate, and it should reflect the knowledge of God. Each element should be simple and clear. There is no need for elaborate rituals and ceremonies, but rather all that is needed is a simple application of biblical prescriptions and descriptions. Those who would come in from outside our community of believers should be able to discern that the worship of God is taking place (1 Cor. 14:9, 23–25), even if they do not know our God. The worship of God should reflect a reverence that is seen in the orderly—not chaotic—presence of his people (1 Cor. 14:33, 40), who are filled with joy and who express his goodness. Appendix 3 presents orders of worship from two predominantly African-American churches that seek to reflect Reformed theology. They are in some points different in emphases, but you will notice that the content and even the form is quite similar.

Something Old, Something New, Everything True

Finally, when we come into worship on the Lord's Day it behooves us to consider the spiritual reality that we do not come alone. We are joined by all those around the world who have received the Lord's summons to come and worship him. Our small corner of our Lord's kingdom may be where we lift our hands and sing our praises, but we must not be so nearsighted as not to see that the church is gathered all around the world. We lift our hands with the church in China, as we do with the church in Canada. We glorify God alongside the redeemed in El Salvador, even as we rejoice with the redeemed in Ethiopia. All around the world God's saints gather on the Lord's Day to say and sing about God what God has said and sung about himself. Yet, as glorious as this thought should be to us, the depth of spiritual realities does not stop there. The congregation with which we sing every Sunday is not just the redeemed from every tribe and tongue upon the earth; we join in with the saints of God who have been made perfect (Heb. 12:23), those already gathered in the heavenly church singing with a perfected praise the glory of our Lord. Every Sunday the saints below join with the saints above to give praise to the risen Lord. When we understand this, when we understand that our worship is represented by those who live now and those who lived before us, it should encourage us to have the old and the new in our worship services.

It is amazing to me that so many churches have implemented two distinct worship services. In this approach, churches hope to appeal to the often conflicting worship styles of the parishioners. To please those of an older generation or taste, churches offer what is known as the traditional worship service. The "contemporary" service is geared toward those of the present generation or those who have a more contemporary taste. More and more churches are implementing this two-service approach in the hopes of attracting, or better yet, keeping more people. While this is not a particularly prevalent occurrence among predominantly black churches, we should be wary of this modern trend and seek to head it off before it reaches our doors.

How deprived we are if all of our songs and forms are contemporary and new. And how shallow and inadequate is our worship if all we have are contemporary music and lyrics. We must remember that Christianity is a "forward remembering" faith. In other words, while we are always looking forward to what God has promised us in the grand consummation, we are always remembering what he did for us at the cross. While we are always proclaiming the glories of the returning King, we are also remembering the glories of the resurrected King. Therefore, let us not jettison the past in favor of the present, and let us not neglect the present in favor of the past. Rather let us embrace them together, even in our worship. How enhanced our worship would be if we made sure that we included such songs as "Joyful, Joyful We Adore Thee" sung to the magnificent arrangement of Beethoven's *Ninth Symphony*, as well as Fred Hammond's "Bread of Life," with its irrepressible urban beats. How glorious and worthy of our God and reflective of heavenly realities would our worship be if we were more diligent in making sure we have something old and something new, yet always careful to maintain all things true.

Admittedly, this is nowhere near an exhaustive treatment of the subject of worship. The Bible has a lot more to say about the Who, what, why, and how of worship than most of us realize. Nevertheless, I do hope you have been able to get a glimpse of how Reformed theology could and should impact a worship service within the predominantly African-American context. I remain convinced that Reformed theology and the African-American Christian experience are not irreconcilable or antithetical. When properly understood and applied together they can form a vision of Christianity, even Christian worship, that would call the angels down to investigate these God-exalting, soul-stirring, hands-lifting, mind-renewing, life-empowering, grace-enabling, sin-overcoming, mercy-receiving, humility-mongering, servant-leading, righteousness-hungering, Bible-believing, Christ-worshiping, eternity-anticipating Christians—who happen also to be black.

5

BIBLICAL SPIRITUALITY
Experiencing the Spirit of God

by KENNETH JONES

Almost without public notice, and with little or no fanfare, a new Black spirituality has moved to center stage and is coloring and affecting everything it touches. The new spirituality, like the old, is rooted in The Great Black Spirit that enabled African-Americans to survive slavery and to change the color of American culture and, some say, American religion. But the new spirituality, like the old, is a growing, teaching thing, and it is evolving, even as we read, seeking its truth, like the old Spirit, in the heavens of our hope.[1]

The above quote is from the December 2004 issue of *Ebony* magazine. The article entitled "The New Black Spirituality" interweaves comments from significant black religious leaders and related articles on issues such as women clergy and the relatively recent rise of black mega-churches. In many respects what is described in the *Ebony* article, as well as in George Barna and Harry R. Jackson's book, *High Impact African-American Churches,* is a change in American evangelicalism as a whole. Wade Clark Roof's *A Generation of Seekers* and *Spiritual Marketplace: Baby Boomers and the Remaking of American Religion* address the rekindled interest in spiritual matters over the last twenty years or so. So the rise of "the new black spirituality," although viewed and contextualized from the perspective of the traditional black church, is really another dimension of the changing face of American evangelicalism.

The Christianity that came to the shores of America in the mid-seventeenth century was largely Calvinistic or reformational in substance. Historian Paul K. Conkin observes, "Thus it is not a great exaggeration to describe colonial religion as at least mildly Calvinistic, for the exceptions were small sects—Quakers, a sprinkling of free-will Baptists, and the German Anabaptist."[2]

Orthodoxy in this setting consisted in the *solas* of the Reformation, the sovereignty of God, the Trinity, the incarnation, sin and depravity, and the sufficiency and centrality of Christ. With the ecumenical creeds the *Canons of Dordt* and the *Book of Common Prayer* as the early standard, Christians in colonial America had a solid base from which they developed catechisms for new converts, the confirmation of children, and overall discipleship in the faith. The pietistic introspective character of colonial Christianity (especially New England Puritanism) notwithstanding, it was largely confessional and doctrinal in character. A person was determined to be a Christian on the basis of adhering to and confessing a particular body of objective truth. With this as a backdrop, we can begin to discuss and understand the introduction of Christianity to the African slaves.

The Introduction of Christianity to Slaves

Initially white slave owners were reluctant to evangelize their slaves. A number of reasons have been offered for this reluctance, chief among them:

1. Slave owners were concerned that if slaves were allowed to become Christians and therefore brothers and sisters in the

faith, they would demand freedom and equal treatment as citizens.

2. Some whites maintained that black Africans were mere brutes, barely above animals, and did not possess a soul, therefore evangelism would be useless.

3. Given the language barrier, some slave owners did not want to take away valuable worktime to establish viable communication necessary to impart the doctrines of the Christian faith.

Let us consider the first two objections to the evangelization of the slaves in more detail. In 1680 the Church of England maintained that slavery and Christianity were compatible. Eventually the colonies drafted legislation denying emancipation to baptized slaves. However, the threat of Christianity bringing emancipation to the slaves being removed still did not prompt slave owners to enthusiastically evangelize and catechize their slaves. Bishop George Berkeley complained about the American colonists in 1731: "ancient antipathy to the Indians . . . together with an irrational contempt for the blacks, as creatures of another species, who had no right to be instructed or admitted to the sacraments, have proved a main obstacle to the conversion of these poor people."[3]

In 1709, Francis Le Jau, a missionary to Goose Creek, South Carolina, reported, "Many masters can't be persuaded that Negroes and Indians are otherwise more than beasts, and use them as such."[4] Edmond Gibson, the Bishop of London, challenged such thinking and exhorted the colonists "to encourage and promote the instruction of their Negroes in the Christian faith" and "to consider them, not merely as slaves, and upon the same level with laboring beasts, but as men-slaves and women-slaves, who have the same frame and faculties with yourselves, and have souls capable of being made eternally happy, and reason and understanding to receive instruction in order to it."[5] The Puritan Cotton Mather in his tract "The Negro Christianized" (1706) argued,

One table of the Ten Commandments has this for the sum of it; Thou shalt love thy neighbor as thy self. Man, thy Negro is thy neighbor.

It were ignorance, unworthy of a man to imagine otherwise. Yea, if thou dost grant that God hath made of one blood, all nations of men; he is thy brother too.[6]

In 1693 Mather organized a Society of Negroes, which met on Sunday evenings to preach to the slaves and to teach them to pray, sing, and recite the Catechism. Eventually other missionary groups such as the Society for the Propagation of the Gospel took on the challenge of evangelizing black slaves.

The Bible and Slavery

It has been noted that Christianity was used by slave owners to make slaves more docile and content in their subjugation. Passages like Ephesians 6:5–8and Colossians 3:22–25 were used to undergird the Church of England's contention that slavery and Christianity were fully compatible. Given the Calvinistic doctrines of predestination and providence, it is easy to see how it could be concluded that:

1. Slavery as an institution was sanctioned by Scripture.
2. Africans were predestined by God to become slaves.
3. God in his providence intended slavery as a means of bringing pagan Africans under the influence of the gospel.

In the first place, it would be quite a stretch to equate American slavery with the slavery in either the Old or New Testaments. Patrick Fairbairn among others has done a solid job in showing that this is an untenable position.[7] As for sanctioning slavery on the basis of the doctrine of predestination, this is much more complex and is probably best understood in light of the more comprehensive subject of theodicy. That the American institution of slavery was evil and contrary to what Scripture teaches concerning one's treatment of one's neighbor is undenied. That God decrees and predetermines all that occurs in the created order is not just an Augustinian or Calvinist conception, it is Scripture. In Isaiah 45:7, the Lord declares, "I form light and create darkness, I make well-being and create calamity; I am the LORD, who does all these things" (see also Isa. 46:9–11). This is a difficult doctrine to be sure, one that non-Reformed Christians have vigorously denied and debated and at times misunderstood. At the same time, some of the doctrine's proponents have misapplied and misrepresented it. This is certainly true of those who would try to commend slavery on the basis of God's decree and providence. Reformed theologian Louis Berkhof in his *Manual of Christian Doctrine* offers this description of the nature of the divine decrees:

> The decree of God is His eternal plan or purpose, in which He has foreordained all things that come to pass. It is but natural that God, who controls all things, should have a definite plan according to which he works, not only in creation and providence, but also in the process of redemption. This plan includes many particulars, and therefore we often speak of the divine decrees in the plural, though in reality there is but a single decree. For the material contents of His decree God drew on the boundless knowledge which He has of all kinds of possible things. Of course this great store of possibilities He embodied in His decree only those things which actually come to pass. Their inclusion in the decree does not necessarily mean that He Himself will actively bring them into existence, but means in some cases that, with the divine permission and according to the divine plan, they will certainly be brought to realization by His rational creatures. The decree covers all the works of God in creation and redemption, and also embraces the actions of His free moral beings, not excluding their sinful actions. But while the entrance of sin into the world and its various manifestations in the lives of angels and men were thus rendered certain, this does not mean that God decided to effectuate these Himself. God's decree with reference to sin is a permissive decree.[8]

Berkhof's description of God's decree and by extension the providential ways in which it is accomplished will not satisfy those who disagree with the Reformed doctrines of predestination and providence. At the same time, agreement with Reformed distinctives does not justify participation in an enterprise that was clearly evil. In other words, the end of evangelism of the slaves does not justify the means of chattel slavery. Peter makes this point in Acts 2:23 when talking about the crucifixion of Christ; that end was according to "the definite plan and foreknowledge of God" but the men who participated in this deed are called "lawless." The point here is that it can justifiably be claimed that through slavery many were exposed to the gospel who may not otherwise have been so. But this neither validates the system nor vindicates the participants in that system.

As I mentioned, predestination is not a welcome doctrine among Christians, black or white, who do not understand or embrace reformational theology. When black Christians hear slavery justified on the grounds of God's eternal decree, they have a tendency to reject the doctrine as the white man's distortion of biblical truth, or worse, some will view this as another reason to reject the "white man's religion" outright. The black eighteenth-century poet Phillis Wheatley seemed to understand this difficult doctrine in reference to slavery. In a poem written in 1768, entitled "On Being Brought from Africa to America," she writes:

> Twas mercy brought me from my pagan land
> Taught my benighted soul to understand
> That there's a God, that there's a Savior too;
> Once I redemption neither sought nor knew.
> Some view our sable race with scornful eye,
> "Their colour is a diabolic die,"
> Remember, Christian, Negro, black as Cain,
> May be refin'd and join th' angelic train.[9]

Henry Louis Gates Jr. says about this poem, "This, it can safely be said, has been the most reviled poem in African-American literature."[10] Yet, far from accepting slavery and all of its inherent cruelties because of the "mercy" that brought knowledge of a Savior, Wheatley, in a letter to a Reverend Samson Occon that was published in the *Connecticut Gazette* on March 11, 1774, wrote:

> In every human breast, God has implanted a principle, which we
> call Love of Freedom; it is impatient of oppression, and pants for

deliverance; and by leave of our modern Egyptians I will assent, that the same principle lives in us. God grant deliverance in his own way in time, and grant his honour upon all those whose avarice implies them to countenance and help the calamities of their fellow creatures. This I desire not for their hurt, but to convince them of the strange absurdity of their conduct whose words and actions are so dramatically opposite. How well the cry for liberty, and the reverse disposition for the exercise of oppressive power over others agree, I humbly think it does not require the Penetration of a philosopher to determine.[11]

As Joseph told his brothers who had faked his death and sold him into slavery, "You meant evil against me; but God meant it for good . . ." (Gen. 50:20).

As previously stated some of the religious instruction of the slaves was slanted to validate their slave status, but Henry Mitchell makes the case that some masters deleted portions of Scripture from the Bibles used to instruct the slaves, such as Moses and the Exodus, for fear of inciting them to seek freedom on the basis of Scripture. If this is true then it is remarkable that Moses and the book of Exodus provided some of the strongest metaphors and imagery that comforted slaves in their plight and that fostered their hope. Harriet Tubman was called "Black Moses" as she transported slaves to freedom in the Underground Railroad. And "Go Down Moses" is one of the most popular Negro spirituals: "Go down Moses, way down in Egypt Land, tell de Pharaoh, let my people go." This brings up the question,what was the content of the religious instruction given to the slaves, once the slave owners were exhorted and encouraged to provide such instruction? (In 1724, a proposal was drafted in Virginia that offered a tax break to those who instructed slaves and brought them to baptism.) In *Slave Religion*, Albert Raboteau gives the report of Ebenezer Taylor, a missionary to St. Andrew's Parish in South Carolina from 1711 to 1717. Taylor commends the efforts of two of his parishioners:

Mrs. Haige and Mrs. Edwards, who came lately to this plantation [Carolina], have taken extra-ordinary pains to instruct a considerable number of Negroes, in the principles of the Christian religion, and to reclaim and reform them. The wonderful success they met with, in about half a year's time, encouraged me to go and examine those Negroes, about their knowledge in Christianity; they declared to me their faith in the chief articles of our religion, which they sufficiently explained; they rehearsed by heart, very distinctly, the Creed, the Lord's Prayer, and Ten Commandments; fourteen of them gave me so great satisfaction, and were so desirous to be baptized, that I thought it my duty to do it on the last Lord's Day.[12]

If this is any indication, it would seem that in spite of efforts to use the Bible to make the slaves more docile, the religious instruction of slaves did include some of the fundamental doctrines of the faith. In fact, the 1724 legislative proposal mentioned above recommended:

It is therefore humbly proposed that every Indian, Negro or Mulatto child that shall be baptized and afterwards brought to church and publicly catechized by the minister and in Church before the 14th year of his or her age, shall give a distinct account of the creed, Lord's Prayer and Ten Commandments.[13]

In 1710 Francis Le Gau indicated that his instruction to Indians and slaves consisted in the same content.

Albert Raboteau makes the claim that the mid 1700s saw an intensive effort on the part of missionaries, ministers, and masters to instruct the slaves on the fundamentals of the faith. In addition to this instruction being undoubtedly skewed at points to subdue any notions of rebellion, it can also be maintained that the motive of some slave owners was not genuine concern for the spiritual well-being of their African slaves. Yet it does seem to be borne out that religiously instructed slaves were exposed to the prevailing orthodoxy of the day.

However, Raboteau and others make the case that in spite of the efforts and a number of slave baptisms, "Christianity touched most slaves indirectly if at all."[14] Henry Mitchell reports "that no significant number of the enslaved were converted to Christianity by white initiative during the so-called 'silent years' from 1619 to 1750."[15] Mitchell goes on to say that, "The fact that Christianity took root at all among African-Americans from 1619 to 1750 is not due to any appreciable measure to missions."[16]

Spiritual Growth in the Slave Community

It might be an overstatement on Mitchell's part to say that white mission endeavors had no "appreciable" impact, but he is correct in saying that the years of 1619 to 1750 were hardly silent as it related to the spiritual development of the African slaves. Mitchell says,

> As soon as enough Africans were imported and settled in a single location, they readily recalled and shared the commonalities of their African religious traditions and engaged once again in an adaptation of their already similar worship practices. Records of their being forbidden to gather clearly establish the fact that, regardless of the variety of tribal backgrounds on any given plantation, they did gather and devoutly engage in an African style of common worship![17]

What Mitchell is alluding to is what has been termed "the invisible institution." This refers to the secret gatherings of slaves on the plantations, away from the watchful eye of the master. Melva Wilson Costen observes:

> In secret gatherings, African descendants risked their lives as they honed and expressed their own beliefs in response to Almighty God. Exposure to the New World environment, New World Christianity, and newly arriving Africans allowed them to contextualize Christianity while being reminded of traditional African religions.[18]

The idea of contextualizing Christianity is important in understanding the African-American religious experience. Ronald Potter has noted, "Evangelicals have sometimes been slow to understand the reality of contextualization of all thought."[19]

From the moment Christian slave owners began to evangelize their African slaves, a different context for the Christian faith was established. Mitchell makes the case that the Africans saw in Christianity resemblances of their native religions. He writes:

> The most important African survivals of all may very well be in the belief systems, African traditional religious doctrines, as closely related to and merged with the orthodox Christian faith. At some points, the parallels are amazing, as with omnipotence, justice, omniscience, and the providence of God. None of these attributes of God had to be learned first in slavery. And all of these crossover African beliefs survived so amazingly well in America because they served so well to support African American psychic survival under oppression.[20]

The invisible institution provided the space and atmosphere to contextualize the message received from missionaries, masters, and white churches against the backdrop of the slaves' own religious heritage. Carl Ellis, in his book *Free at Last* observes:

> Slave master Christianity-ism was rejected by most Christian slaves, but under its cover they began to develop an indigenous theological outlook and practice. Because slaves were not allowed to meet together without the presence of whites, they began using double-meaning language. When the master was present in black worship, he would think the slaves were singing and shouting about one thing (spiritual freedom perhaps) when in reality they were thinking of another (freedom this side of heaven).[21]

So even though their white instructors of religion slanted the biblical message to keep the slaves docile and content in their enslaved status, the slaves themselves took what they learned, and in the confines of the invisible institution contextualized it to nurture a deep-rooted faith and hope. Twentieth-century black radicals would claim that the slaves were brainwashed with the white man's religion so that their hope was in "pie in the sky, in the sweet by-and-by." But a closer examination of the facts reveals that while this might have been the intention, it was far from the case. Such a view underestimates the slaves' ability to read between the lines of what they heard and what they saw. As they heard the biblical narratives preached in the invisible institution, they trusted that the God who delivered Daniel from the lion's den and the Hebrew boys from the fiery furnace would deliver them as well. As Juan Williams and Quinton Dixie note in *This Far by Faith*:

> And when black people came to white Christian churches, there was little Christian grace. Blacks often had to sit in the back, in the balcony, or even outside. In some cases they had to attend separate services. This perversion of Christian fellowship only added to the difficulty of black people embracing Christianity. But somehow it did not stop them from believing that the God of Christianity was their God too, and the problem was not with God, his church, or his word in the bible. Faith said the problem was white racism. Black people could have turned against the white Christian church, but instead they separated the message of Christian love from the people who had no love for them.[22]

It was this separation process that allowed the slaves in their makeshift, clandestine worship services to see their plight in the sufferings and rejection of Christ and in the narratives of Israel's bondage in Egypt and Babylon. These services were marked by a sense of freedom, hope, and community. There was freedom of expression in joyful exultation that was not allowed when they attended white churches; they had the freedom to sing and dance in celebration before God. They sang the hymns of the master (with their own flavor) as well as spirituals of their own making. The slaves had hope that just as God delivered Israel from Egypt and Christ from the grave, he would deliver them from their bondage and oppression. The invisible institution also provided community. Slave owners were skeptical of too much fraternizing among the slaves, fearing that uprisings and escape would be the topic of conversation. Most of the permitted socializing was overseen by whites or by slaves that could be trusted to report any talk of insurrection. Worship in the invisible institution offered slaves the opportunity to socialize beyond the master's view and to offer words of comfort to those who had been beaten or had had a loved one sold. They could pray for one another and discuss issues of common concern.

That the catechetical orthodoxy received from white Christians was contextualized by the slaves and mixed with elements of their native religions seems to be an obvious conclusion. Therefore it would be a mistake to assume that all of the religious activities of the slaves during the "silent years" were simply their own expressions of their Christian faith. The fact is many of the catechized slaves during this period simply were not Christian. Raboteau points out that some "interpreted Christianity to fit the world views inherited from their African past."[23] Others simply rejected the Christian message outright. So the invisible institution was an eclectic religious environment, with genuine Christian converts (some weak and some strong) in the faith, as well as practitioners of altered forms of the old religions. W. E. B. DuBois, writing on the evolving spirituality of the African slaves, seems to have had the invisible institution in mind:

> Thus, as bard, physician, judge, and priest, within the narrow limits allowed by the slave system, rose the Negro preacher, and under him the first Afro-American institution, the Negro church. This church was not at first by any means Christian nor definitely organized; rather it was an adaptation of mingling of heathen rites among the members of each plantation, and roughly designated as Voodooism. Association with the masters, missionary effort and motives of expediency gave these rites an early veneer of Christianity, and after the lapse of many generations the Negro Church became Christian.[24]

If Dubois is accurate in his depiction of the invisible institution, it experienced a gradual evolution; it was at first African in content and character, but due to the influence of the Christian message variously received, it became more Christian in content, even as it retained some of its African character and tone.

Black Conversions and the First Great Awakening

In the mid 1700s revival broke out in the New England colonies and eventually made its way to the South. This period of religious fervor became known as the Great Awakening, spearheaded by Jonathan

Edwards, a Congregationalist, Gilbert Tennent, a Presbyterian, and George Whitefield, an Anglican. Despite strict Calvinism of these renowned preachers, this period of revival featured unusual emotional responses on the part of the listeners. Edwards, in particular, was concerned about some of the extremities associated with what he saw as a genuine outpouring of the Holy Spirit in making men sensible of their sins and of the saving grace of God in the person and work of Jesus Christ. As much as he was convinced that this was a legitimate work of God, he was also aware of and concerned about the illegitimacy of the acts of some of those caught up in the moment. This prompted him in 1735 to write *Narratives of Surprising Conversions*. Later he would publish *The Distinguishing Marks of a Work of the Spirit of God*, *Thoughts on the Revival*, and *The Religious Affections*.

The zeal sometimes manifest in great emotional displays associated with the revival meetings, including bodily convulsions, caught the attention of the slaves. Edwards, Whitefield, and Tennent were all surprised to see Negroes attending these meetings. This emotionally charged atmosphere was not typical of what took place in the white churches they attended with their masters, but it was reminiscent of worship in the invisible institution. This made the black slaves feel (perhaps for the first time) more a part of what was going on. Shouting and crying out loud, which would have been frowned on in the white church proper, was now done openly, as black and white listeners were moved by the praying and preaching. Mitchell writes:

> The spontaneous expressiveness fostered by the preaching of George Whitefield and others in the First Great Awakening led to an enormous increase of African public commitment to the Christian faith. The ecstasy experienced in traditional slave worship could now be publicly affirmed as authentically Christian at the same time.[25]

Whitefield, who was known for his thunderous voice and dramatic flair, was a particular favorite among the slaves. Mitchell quotes a black hearer of Whitefield's preaching:

When I got into the church, I saw this pious man exhorting the people with the greatest fervor and earnestness, and sweating as much as I ever did while in slavery on Monteserrat beach. . . . I was very much struck and impressed with this; I thought it strange that I had never seen divines exert themselves in this manner before.[26]

Vernon Loggins says of the black response to revivalist preachers:

The Christianity which Whitefield and his predecessors preached in America brought to the Negro a religion which he could understand, and which could stir him to self-expression. He responded to it with enthusiasm.[27]

This parallels what Raboteau says about the second Great Awakening (which we will address later):

While the Anglican clergymen tended to be didactic and moralistic, the Methodist or Baptist exhorted, visualized and personalized the drama of sin and salvation, of damnation and election.[28]

The Anglicans usually taught the slaves the Ten Commandments, the Apostles' Creed, and the Lord's Prayer. The revivalist preacher helped them to feel the weight of sin, to imagine the threats of hell, and to accept Christ as their only Savior. The enthusiasm of the camp meeting, as excessive as it seemed to some churchmen, was triggered by the preacher's personal, emotional appeal and the common response of members of his congregation. The revivalists tended, moreover, to minimize doctrine. The importance of the atmosphere and preaching style of the revivals in attracting slaves to openly embrace Christianity cannot be overstated.

Another thing that may have contributed to the explosion of black conversions during the Great Awakening, was the genuine compassion shown to the slaves by some of its greatest preachers. John Wesley, for his part, wrote *Thoughts upon Slavery*, with scathing indictments against Christian participation in the institution. Contrary to the likes of Cotton Mather and even the revivalist Jonathan Edwards, who saw it as their duty to evangelize the slaves yet were themselves slave owners, Wesley strongly denounced the whole system.

George Whitefield is a different and more complex story. Whitefield was outraged at the treatment of black slaves throughout the South and eventually wrote an open letter to denounce their ill-treatment. Along with William Seward, Whitefield bought five thousand acres of land in unoccupied, uncleared country on the forks of the Delaware River. The plan was to build a school for Negroes and establish a colony of Christian immigrants from England. They christened the land Nazareth and envisioned it being an outpost of reconciliation, where Negroes would learn in freedom, and white and black together could evangelize the Indians. This colony never quite materialized, although Whitefield was adored and much loved by blacks everywhere he went. They not only loved his preaching, but they loved the man. However, though Whitefield opposed the treatment of slaves, he did not see the institution as being inconsistent with Christianity, and he was influential in bring slavery into Georgia. Whitefield eventually became a slave owner himself. One of his biographers, John Pollock, writes:

> His slaves were the best treated, the happiest in the entire South; he even brought out a young man to look after their spiritual and temporal interests. The Negroes loved George Whitefield.[29]

Whitefield is not to be excused for his shortsightedness on this issue, and he is certainly not to be lauded as a hero for opposing the greater evil of brutality against the slaves while upholding a system that was in itself inhuman. What cannot be denied are the genuine affection engendered by his kindness to slaves in general and his commitment to their spiritual and educational development. The character and compassion of preachers like Wesley and Whitefield was a significant factor in blacks' converting to Christianity.

A third factor in the conversion of large numbers of blacks during the revivals of the First Great Awakening was that these revivals allowed participation in public prayer and proclamation by those that would ordinarily not be permitted to do so in a church setting.

This included blacks. One critic noted, "Indeed young persons, sometimes lads, or rather boys, nay women and girls, yea Negroes, have taken upon them to do the business of preaching."[30] This public participation, like the expressiveness, was something that the white churches largely denied and was undoubtedly a factor in the widespread embrace of Christianity during the revivals.

Effects of the Second Great Awakening

Most historians acknowledge that the effects of the First Great Awakening began to wane by 1744, and that the second Great Awakening began in 1787 at Hampden-Sydney and Washington colleges. The 1801 camp meeting in Cane Ridge, Kentucky, marks the real launching of the second significant period of revival in America. Most historians will also note that although the Cane Ridge camp meeting began in the Presbyterian church, ultimately this period of revival spawned significant changes in the theological underpinning of the whole of American evangelicalism. However, I would maintain that the seeds of theological change that blossomed in the Second Great Awakening were planted in the First Great Awakening and were watered in the theological controversy in the interim.

The controversy that I am referring to is the "New Light" controversy, which resulted from the emotional enthusiasm of the First Great Awakening. Traditional Presbyterians and Congregationalists, dubbed "Old Light," understood their Calvinism in rationalistic terms. They maintained that holding orthodox theology, not subjective experience or personal piety, was the basis of true Christian profession. The "New Lighters" preached the need to have an experiential conviction of sin and a pursuit of piety in order for one to claim to be a Christian. Like the seventeenth-century German Pietists, the New Lighters charged the Old Lighters with formalism that engages the head but not the heart. The enormous success of the First Great Awakening revivals gave the New Lighters momentum, and in its wake a strong emphasis on a conversion experience became dominant. Mitchell makes the point that the stress on conviction and sorrow for sin strongly paralleled the African belief system, thereby providing another appeal to black religious sensibilities.

In short, the First and Second Great Awakenings were appealing to blacks for a number of reasons, and therefore were the impetuses for them openly embracing the Christian religion in greater numbers. Furthermore, these revivals brought significant changes in American evangelicalism as a whole. This is especially the case with the Second Great Awakening. While the content of the preaching in the First Great Awakening was largely Calvinistic (with the exception of the Wesleys), the style was dramatic and fervent. This emotional fervor was even stronger during the Second Great Awakening, as were the demonstrative responses to the preaching. However, by the time the Second Great Awakening has reached its apex, the preaching (spearheaded by Charles Finney) content was decidedly different from the Calvinism of the first. The emphasis shifted from the sovereignty of God to the ability of man. Wesleyan piety and perfectionism, coupled with Finney's revival methods and theological twists, paved a new path for American evangelicalism.

Black Spirituality and Theology

With this historical overview of the theological influences surrounding and shaping the Christian faith, introduced to the slaves, and contextualized in the invisible institution, we return to the issue of "black spirituality."

It is apparent that theology and doctrine are not the means by which "black spirituality" is distinguished, for the most part, from any other type. One notable exception to this would be the adherents to "black theology" proper. It is clear from some of the contributors to Linda E. Thomas's *Living Stones in the Household of God: The Legacy and Future of Black Theology* that proponents and practitioners of "black theology" have, through re-reading and re-interpreting the Bible, made a conscious departure from the ideological presuppositions of what James Cones has called "Euro-American theology."[31] Black spirituality from the perspective of "black theology" is more than just our unique soulful flavoring of historic Christianity. It is doing theology from a different starting point ("oppression and suffering" as opposed to creation, the fall, and original sin), and with a different aim (to seek the liberation of the oppressed). But this is not the position of most African-American Christians, regardless of the fact that many black churches consciously or otherwise preserve the tone and tenor of "black churchism."

I think it would be safe to say that the majority of black churches still adhere to the basic tenets and theological presuppositions of the varying strands of American evangelicalism. This includes the good, the bad, and the ugly evangelical theology with a host of off-shoots. What I mean is that "black churchism" is being played out against the backdrops of liberal theology, Lutheranism, Calvinism, feminism, social gospel, Armenianism, prosperity gospel, seeker sensitive worship, and the mega-church movement. When *Ebony* magazine speaks of "The New Black Spirituality," it is really describing the participation of black Christians and churches in the trends and methods that seem to be dominating the American religious scene. It is my contention that these trends are evidence of a theological and philosophical shift from historical Protestantism. Many have written about this shift over the years, and many continue to sound the alarm that we are headed into dangerous waters as we drift further and further away from the doctrinal harbors of our Protestant forefathers. In fact, some would even say that we are no longer drifting, but have landed on an island of man-centered, subjective, relativistic, post-modern, neo-gnostic spirituality, which we have presumptuously called Christianity.

The subtitle of Brian D. Mclaren's *A Generous Orthodoxy* makes my point: *Why I Am a Missional + Evangelical + Post/Protestant + Liberal/Conservative + Mystical/Poetic + Biblical + Charismatic/ Contemplative + Fundamentalist/Calvinist + Anabaptist/Anglican + Methodist + Catholic + Green + Incarnation + Depressed-Yet-Hopeful + Emergent + Unfinished Christian.* For better or worse, this is where we are; denominational and doctrinal distinctives have been cast aside, and we are left with a buffet of methods, principles, trends, and formulas masquerading as Christianity. Some see this as a good thing, others see it as not necessarily good, but as the inevitable tide of progress. So while some may not agree with or understand the changes, they do not want to be considered irrelevant or out-of-touch with the times. But others see the shift as a dangerous compromise that undermines the faith.

Francis Schaeffer stands as a modern prophet in this movement with a number of challenging works, most notably the *Great Evangelical Disaster*. In a similar vein is the *Scandal of the Evangelical Mind*, by Mark Noll; *God in the Wasteland*, by David Wells and his equally challenging *Above All Earthly Powers; Made in America*, by Michael Horton; and *The Coming Evangelical Crisis*, edited by John Armstrong.[32] All of these writers address the fact that American evangelicalism has lost its theological/doctrinal, intellectual, philosophical, and moral footing. In light of the sentiments of these and other writers of the same ilk, I contend that evangelical Christians need to re-examine or perhaps rediscover the parameters of our faith. In other words, we need to return to the substance of the creeds, confessions, and catechisms that carefully articulate and outline what we believe the Bible to teach for faith and practice. Our demise is not that the Bible is not being taught, but that it is being taught without doctrinal precision, theological categories, or a christological center. The historic standards do not supplant that authority of Holy Scripture as previous generations supposed (hence the fundamentalist charge of "no creed but Christ, no book but the Bible").

We have had more than 150 years of this sort of thinking, and it has slowly produced a brand of Christianity commonly described as a mile wide and an inch deep. The width would explain the swelling numbers of churchgoers and professing Christians, but the depth (or lack thereof) would explain the shallowness of our understanding of the most basic Christian doctrines. Harold Bloom (who was not a Christian) noted, "So creedless is the American religion that it needs to be tracked by particles rather than by principles."[33]

Contrary to what some may think, creeds and confessions are not rivals to the authority of Scripture, rather they are guides that help us navigate the Scriptures and come away with a clear and consistent faith. As creeds, confessions, and catechisms have been thrown to the side, what has taken center stage is a Christianity that for all intents and purposes resembles pop psychology and pop culture more that it does historic Christianity. Historic Protestant confessions and catechisms tell us of the threefold office of Christ as Prophet, Priest, and King. Contemporary Christianity presents a Jesus that was a great teacher and moral example. Our confessions tell us what God has done for wretched sinners in the person and work of Christ, through careful statements on justification, imputation, the atonement, sanctification, and glorification. Contemporary Christianity asks us, what would Jesus do? The creeds declare that Jesus was wholly God and wholly man. At least one contemporary preacher says that Mary (the mother of Christ) was an at-risk teenage mother. How many Christians think that suicide will land a person in hell because the person did not have time to ask for forgiveness? Or how many Christians are looking or working for an anointing, because they don't realize that "the anointing" is upon Christ and, by virtue of our union with Christ, what is his is ours, so that as 1 John 2:20 expresses it, "But you have been anointed by the Holy One. . . ." Rugged individualism might be the stuff from which the American dream is forged, but it is disastrous when it comes to the Christian faith. While John Armstrong observes that "the shape that modern evangelicalism has taken over the last few decades makes it increasingly less Protestant,"[34] Peter Jones and James A. Herick depict an evangelicalism that is increasingly less Christian.[35]

Evangelicalism and the Black Church

What does all of this have to do with "black spirituality"? Everything, because once you get beyond the veneer of cultural character and ethnic flavoring, what is being practiced in black churches is our own version of the various strands of evangelicalism in other churches. Whether it be the antebellum black church, the black churches that grew out of the Second Great Awakening, or the black church during the civil rights era, we have always held to the same theological/doctrine presuppositions of some brand of white evangelicalism. Our emphasis may have been (necessarily) overtly social because of our social status, but our theology has generally reflected that of our white denominational counterparts. This may seem to be a superfluous point to make, but I make it for two reasons. First, if we are talking about Christianity when speaking of "black spirituality," we are referring to a distinction of style, context, and character, as opposed to a difference in substance and content. Second, I want to remind black Christians that the problems of American evangelicalism are our problems as well. In light of this I offer the following challenges and concerns.

First, as African-American Christians we must see ourselves in the lineage of historic Protestantism. We have celebrated our ethnic heritage, and we have made a conscious effort to remember our history of suffering and oppression. We hold in high esteem the names of Harriet Tubman, Nat Turner, Sojourner Truth, Absolam Jones, and Richard Allen. But just as these men and women made significant contributions to our hard-fought freedom, we need to recognize the individuals who have contributed to defining, defending, and declaring our most precious faith; individuals like Augustine, Athanasius, Anselm, Martin Luther, John Calvin, John Owen, John Flavel, Thomas Boston, J. Gresham Machen, Jonathan Edwards, and Francis Turretin. It is not enough for our ministers to learn of these men in seminary; the labors of these men benefit the whole body. They are no more perfect than our black heroes, but their contributions are no less significant to our faith. Black spirituality, if it is Christian, needs to be nourished by the sages of the church whatever their race or ethnicity. Church history is our history, and ignorance of that history and those who have contributed to it is our loss.

A few years ago when major league baseball was celebrating the fiftieth anniversary of Jackie Robinson breaking the color line, a sportswriter interviewed a number of black ballplayers, asking their feelings on the significance of what Robinson did and its benefits to black players that followed him. I was startled when one young black superstar claimed he didn't know who Jackie Robinson was. I hope he was making a poor attempt at humor or was claiming ignorance because he didn't want to do the interview. But if he truly didn't know who Jackie Robinson was, it is tragic that he could become a millionaire because of the courage of a man that he doesn't know about. But how much more tragic it is for black or white Christians to be ignorant of Martin Luther and his *Ninety-Five Theses* or Calvin and his *Institutes of the Christian Religion*. Are we content to cite the fact that Athanasius and Augustine were African and not impart their rich teaching?

Second, we as African-American Christians must guard against rejecting God's commandment so that we may keep the tradition of men, which Jesus speaks of in Mark 7:9. Have we substituted the "how" of worship for the "what"? Many black Christians are suspicious of a church where the preacher doesn't "whoop" or the choir doesn't rock the house or people do not "shout," because these are the things associated with a genuine black worship experience. Whatever the origins of our unique expressiveness, is this what we have come to? Have we allowed all manner of error and heresy to enter our churches as we have tenaciously guarded our manner of expression? Consider that we may overestimate the importance of the traditional emotional fervor of the black worship experience for many black worshippers.

In the early 1970s Fred Price of the Crenshaw Christian Center in Los Angeles became popular by consciously eschewing not only the message of traditional black preaching, but also the method. Price stood with an open Bible and in even, measured tones, expounded his particular doctrine. I've had a number of former Crenshaw Christian Center members acknowledge that part of what drew them in the first place was that Pastor Price actually preached in a way that they could understand. The numerical growth of Price's church came at the expense of many traditional black churches of every denomination. But there were also those who would attend the early services at Crenshaw and then go to the later service at their traditional church. In fact I have encountered a number of black Christians who get their "teaching" from other sources—radio teachers, conferences, books, etc.—but go to "traditional" black churches to "get their praise on." I was at a conference once that featured white theologians as the keynote speakers. During a break, I ran into a fellow black pastor whom I was acquainted with. I asked what he thought of the speaker. He responded by saying, "Man, that was some good stuff, but if he ever preached in a black church he would have to bring it better than that." On the one hand Fred Price, whose congregation, although mixed, is predominantly black, has disproved that theory. But on the other hand this brother typified the very real but hard to document problem of black traditionalism hindering the development of biblical spirituality.

Let me offer two qualifications. First, the above mentioned problem of cultural traditionalism overshadowing biblical spirituality is not unique to the black church. It would be the same problem with any church where one ethnic group is dominant. Korean, Latin, Dutch, and German friends have expressed the same concerns. The manifestations will differ but the problem is the same. Second, our cultural traditions and flavoring are not necessarily antithetical to biblical spirituality. In other words, "how we do church" is not wrong or bad in and of itself. The problem is that the "how" in many instances has become an end unto itself. Preachers whoop for the purpose of whooping, and worshippers are enticed to shout for the sake of shouting. Or what's worse is that one is made to think that if you do not join the fervor there is something wrong with your spirituality. Furthermore, preachers are made to think that evoking a verbal response is proof of having preached a good sermon. If this is what we are calling and celebrating as black spirituality, serious questions ought to be raised.

I began this chapter by surveying the evolution and contextualizing of the Christian faith among African-Americans. At the same time I've tried to make the point that American Christianity itself has undergone many shifts and changes. Some of these changes have been for the good; this is especially true on social and racial issues. We are far from perfect in race relations within the body of Christ, but we are far from the polarizing and poisoned position in the early and middle decades of the last century. While we continue to make strides in the area of social and racial issues, it seems we are losing ground in the area of doctrinal and theological clarity. Doctrine is being undermined. This is a problem for all who name the name of Christ. As Christian faith and practice has been usurped by postmodern relativistic thinking, therapeutic methods, marketing techniques, and neo-gnostic spirituality, we need to return to the standards of historic Protestantism. These confessions, creeds, and catechisms are tried, true, biblical, and helpful to clearly and consistently express what we believe. The social and moral issues of our day are complex and far-reaching, but with these challenges we are still ambassadors of Christ, appointed to be his witnesses in this present age. Let us therefore "examine ourselves as to whether we are in the faith," so that our witness will be true, consistent, and biblical.

Biblical Spirituality

So what is biblical spirituality? To answer this we will consider man in creation, man in the fall, and man in regeneration. In this regard Reformed theology is most helpful in presenting a clear and biblically consistent view of what we have been saved from and what we have been saved for.

What We Have Been Saved From

Genesis 1:26–31 and 2:7 record God's creation of man. Man was created in the image of God. James Boice summarizes man's being created in God's image as consisting in three elements: personality, morality, and spirituality. "To have personality one must possess knowledge, feelings (including religious feelings) and a will. Morality includes the two further elements of freedom and responsibility."[36] This is not an absolute freedom, as if Adam and Eve were autonomous beings. This simply means they were not constrained internally or externally from doing what they were commanded to do. Furthermore, the eventual disobedience of Adam and Eve was without compulsion.

Man's spirituality consists in qualities such as truth, holiness, and righteousness. As a moral being, man is accountable to his Creator in terms of obeying his commandments. As a moral being who is spiritual, man was created for fellowship and communion with his

Creator. But then came the fall. As the *Baptist Confession of Faith* (1689) states:

> Our first parents, by this sin, fell from their original righteousness and communion with God, and we in them, whereby death came upon all; all becoming dead in sin, and wholly defiled in all the faculties and parts of souls and body.[37]

This is a concise statement of the Reformed doctrine of total depravity. All of Adam's posterity fell in him and with him. It was as if we were all present in the garden participating in the rebellion of our foreparents. The effect of that act was that the image of God was "wholly defiled." Total depravity does not mean that men and women are individually as wicked as they can be, but that each individual is corrupt or defiled in all of his parts. The Bible describes the sinful, fallen state of man as being "dead in the trespasses and sins" (Eph. 2:1; see Col. 2:13). This describes our inability to respond to God's law as we ought. Man still possesses rationality, some sense of morality, and a sense of spirituality, but all of this has been corrupted in the fall; therefore the Bible speaks of our understanding being "darkened" and our hearts being blinded (Eph. 4:18). This means that in our fallen state, both our affections and our thoughts are corrupt and are not in accordance with what God requires. We are still capable of some social good, moral behavior, and even religious activity. But as Isaiah 64:6 expresses it, our righteousness is "like a polluted garment." It is from this sinful state that our sinful deeds flow. The *Baptist Confession* states:

> From this original corruption, whereby we are utterly indisposed, disabled, and made opposite to all good, and wholly inclined to all evil, do proceed all actual transgressions. We do not become sinners when we sin, we sin because we are born in a sinful and corrupt state (Ps. 51:5).[38]

The penalty for our sinful condition is death (Rom. 6:23). If we were able to pay the penalty for our sins, we would then be obligated to perfectly obey God's holy law, in thought, word, and deed, for the rest of our lives. This presents a problem, because if we were able to pay the penalty for our sins, we still would be unable to perform the righteousness required. But God is gracious. He sent his Son to perform the righteousness required in the law and to die for the penalty we owed. Furthermore, Christ is resurrected and is seated at the right hand of the Father. Just as Adam was our covenant head, so that his guilt was our guilt, and we were identified in him, so Christ is our *new* covenant head: his righteousness is our righteousness, and we are identified in him. God awakens dead sinners by the Holy Spirit (Eph. 2:1; John 3:5–8) so that they are aware of their condition and of the saving grace of God in Jesus Christ (1 Cor. 2:7–16). In addition, he gives the gift of faith whereby we embrace Christ and all that he has done for us. This new consciousness of our condition and of God's grace is called regeneration, because it is a new principle of life within us:

> Man, by his fall into a state of sin, hath wholly lost all ability of will to any spiritual good accompanying salvation; so as a natural man, being altogether averse from that good, and dead in sin, is not able by his own strength to convert himself, or to prepare himself thereunto.
>
> When God converts a sinner, and translates him into the state of grace, he freeth him from his natural bondage under sin, and by his grace alone enables him freely to will and to do that which is spiritually good. . . .[39]

In regeneration, sinners are brought into a state of justification whereby they are reconciled to God. Justification means that God declares sinners to be righteous on the basis of Christ's imputed righteousness (Rom. 3:24–26). Regeneration is the work of the Holy Spirit through the Word of God (1 Pet. 1:23), in which the regenerated person is passive. Through the gift of faith we are enabled to repent and lay hold of the grace of God in the person and work of Christ. Berkhof says this of regeneration, "God is the author of regeneration. It is represented in Scripture as the Holy Spirit directly and exclusively. . . ."[40]

This means that in regeneration, only God works, and there is no cooperation of the sinner in this work whatever. So regeneration is not the fruit of faith, rather faith is the fruit of regeneration. This is the beginning of biblical spirituality, when dead sinners are awakened and made responsive to the Word of God and brought into communion with him.

There is much more that I could address, such as election, effectual calling, and the covenants of works and of grace. My purpose has been to outline in broad terms the spiritual vitality we possessed and lost in Adam, the utter inability to properly respond to God in our fallen state, and the new life that we have in Christ.

What We Have Been Saved For

In Ephesians 2:10 the apostle Paul says, "We are his workmanship, created in Christ Jesus for good works, which God prepared beforehand, that we should walk in them." Titus 2:14 says, "Who gave himself for us to redeem us from all lawlessness and to purify for himself a people for his own possession who are zealous for good works." Jesus summarized these good works in this manner: "You shall love the Lord your God with all your heart and with all your soul and with all your mind. This is the great and first commandment. And a second is like it: You shall love your neighbor as yourself. On these two commandments depend all the Law and the Prophets" (Matt. 22:37–40). This is what is meant by the two tables of the law: our duty and devotion to God, and our duty to our neighbor.

We have been saved from the condemnation and corruption that we fell into in Adam. We have been saved by the sovereign power of God, which is a manifestation of his grace and is appropriated by faith (which is also a gift of God.) We have been saved for good works. The *Baptist Confession* says:

> These good works, done in obedience to God's commandments, are the fruits and evidences of a true and lively faith; and by them believers manifest their thankfulness, strengthen their assurance, edify their brethren, and adorn the profession of the gospel, stop the mouths of the adversaries and glorify God.[41]

Biblical spirituality therefore is the transformation of sinners from condemnation to justification, from children of wrath and darkness to children of light, from death to life in Christ by the Holy Spirit. Just how this spirituality is displayed and played out is presented in the New Testament; it affects every area of our lives.

Church. Contrary to the thinking of some, church life is a vital part of our spirituality. As Paul establishes in Ephesians 4:13–16, church is where we have the Word of God preached and taught so that we "attain to the unity of the faith and of the knowledge of the Son of God, to mature manhood, to the measure of the stature of the fullness of Christ, so that we may no longer be children, tossed to and fro by the waves and carried about by every wind of doctrine, by human cunning, by craftiness in deceitful schemes." The pastoral ministry of the church is the means by which God feeds us and brings us to maturity in his Word. This preaching/teaching element in the church is a vital work of the Spirit and is therefore part of our spiritual formation. Ephesians 5:18–21 suggests that formal and corporate worship is also part of that spiritual formation. And 1 Corinthians 11:17–34 illustrates how the Lord's Supper is vital in our spiritual development. But there is another dimension of the corporate church that is a part of our spiritual formation: our interaction with our brothers and sisters in the faith. Ephesians 4:16 says, "the whole body, joined and held together by every joint with which it is equipped, when each part is working properly, makes the body grow so that it builds itself up in love." Or, consider Hebrews 10:24, "And let us consider how to stir up one another to love and good works." It is with this admonition that the writer goes on to say, "not neglecting to meet together, as is the habit of some, but encouraging one another, and all the more as you see the Day drawing near" (Heb. 10:25). Drawing from one another in church fellowship with our brothers and sisters in the faith is an underappreciated dynamic of our spirituality. In fact Paul says that our spiritual gifts are given for "the common good" (1 Cor. 12:7).

Home. Another realm in which our spirituality is displayed and developed is the home. In Reformed circles, much emphasis is placed on covenant families. While I do not agree with all of the implications of the term "covenant families" (i.e. infant baptism), it does rest on a solid understanding of Scripture. The Christian home is to be a place where God is revered and glorified as his grace and love are displayed in us. In 1 Timothy 3, the qualifications for both an elder and a deacon involve the home life of the one seeking the office. There should not only be prayer and devotion in the home, but the home and its activities should be governed by God's Word. In Ephesians 5:22–32 the apostle Paul outlines the roles and responsibilities of Christian wives and husbands, and in 6:1–4 he addresses the relationship between children and their parents. Our spiritual formation includes our being strengthened by the Spirit to reflect the grace and glory of the Savior in the home as well as the church. In Luke 8 we are told of the man from whom Jesus cast out a legion of demons. We read, "The man from whom the demons had gone begged that he might be with him, but Jesus sent him away, saying, 'Return to your home, and declare how much God has done for you'" (vv. 38–39).

The Workplace. The sixteenth-century Protestant Reformation was significant at a number of levels. Not only did it re-establish the apostolic doctrines of salvation by grace through faith in the person and work of Christ and the authority of Scripture, but the Protestant Reformation also established the sacredness of human vocation. In contrast to the notion that evolved out of the monastic movement—that secular vocations were somehow less spiritual than church or religious work—the Reformers affirmed that all work is sacred before God. Man was created to work, as seen in the creation mandate to work and keep the garden of Eden (Gen. 2:15). All work that is not immoral has dignity, because in it man glorifies his Creator by carrying out his created purpose. The apostle Paul issues a severe warning against those who refuse to work in 2 Thessalonians 3:6–12, and in 1 Timothy 5:8 he says that those who do not provide for their families are worse than an unbeliever.

The Reformers not only stressed the dignity of an individual's labor, but they made the point that labor was a means of serving God and humanity. One did not have to serve God solely through religious service, but all labor was unto the Lord: "Whatever you do, work heartily, as for the Lord and not for men, knowing that from the Lord you will receive the inheritance as your reward. You are serving the Lord Christ" (Col. 3:23–24). This is something that contemporary Christians, particularly in the West, should really take to heart: our spirituality extends to our earthly vocations. On the one hand many Christians have been seduced by the spirit of the age, so that dignity is ascribed to high-paying jobs and high-profile careers. Sanitation workers, janitors, and other "blue collar" workers are not held in the same esteem as the more glamorous professions. But if anyone should understand the value and dignity of all honest labor, it should be Christians.

On the other hand, Christians need to be more conscientious of glorifying God in the workplace, and I don't mean in terms of passing out tracts or conducting lunchtime Bible studies. How does one glorify God on the job? By coming to work on time and returning from lunch and breaks on time; by being respectful and submissive to those in authority; by doing one's job with care and excellence; by not stealing office supplies or falsifying expense reports. These things may not sound very spiritual, but in these things we glorify God and serve him.

Citizenship. I am using the term "citizenship" in an overarching way to encompass both our relationship to government and our interactions with our neighbors in a general sense. According to the *Baptist Confession*:

> God, the supreme Lord and King of all the world, hath ordained civil magistrates to be under him, over the people, for his own glory and the public good; and to this end hath armed them with the power of the sword, for defense and encouragement of them that do good, and for the punishment of evil doers. . . .[42]

It goes on to say:

> Civil magistrates being set up by God for the ends aforesaid; subjection, in all lawful things commanded by them, ought to be yielded by us in the Lord, not only for wrath, but for conscience sake, and we ought to make supplications and prayers for kings and all that are in authority, that under them we may live a quiet and peaceable life, in all godliness and honesty.[43]

Among the prooftexts for these paragraphs are Romans 13:1–7, 1 Peter 2:17, and 1 Timothy 2:1–2. The topic of Christians and politics is touchy to say the least. It is not my intention to address specific issues, but to make the point that our living out our faith and being credible witnesses of our Savior is to be guided by Scripture in our dealings in this area.

1. We are to render due honor, respect, and obedience to those who govern, not on the condition that they are "good Christians," but because they are appointed ministers of God (Rom. 13:1–2).

2. We are to pray for those who govern (1 Tim. 2:1–2).

3. We are to draw the line on our submission if and when the government forbids what God has commanded or commands what God forbids (Acts 4:18–31).

4. We are to seek the peace and well-being of the nation (1 Pet. 2:13–17; Col. 4:5–6; Heb. 12:14). However, Christians need not uncritically embrace all that the government does. As a corporate body we have the responsibility to be a prophetic voice against all unrighteousness, including corrupt governing authority. The church is not overstepping its bounds in denouncing the evils in the land that have been given legal sanction, such as abortion and same-sex marriage. As private citizens, Christians are free to voice their dissent on various issues through any number of means allowed by the Constitution and that are not contradictory to the Word of God. We are allowed peaceful protests, and we should voice our concerns to elected officials. Christians have a dual citizenship in this world. We are citizens of the kingdom of God and are governed

by his Word through the church. We are also citizens of an earthly kingdom and are subject to the laws of the land. Although both kingdoms are extensions of God's sovereign rule, they are distinct; failure to recognize the distinction has been and continues to be a source of great confusion for many Christians. On the one hand, churches have become political platforms, espousing the agenda of a particular party. On the other hand, churches have taken on the task of trying to Christianize the culture and its institutions. Either extreme is destined to fail and obscures the dynamics of biblical spirituality as it relates to government.

The other dimension of our citizenship in which our spirituality is lived out is in our relationships and interactions with those outside the church. As Christians, we have the responsibility to share the gospel with all people, but evangelism per se is not our only duty. The summation of the second table of the law is to love our neighbor as ourselves. As Jesus illustrates in the parable of the good Samaritan, our neighbor is not limited to our next-door neighbor, or to a person of the same ethnicity or social class. Biblical spirituality manifests itself in neighborly love. This means, in short, showing respect for all mankind because they are fellow image bearers of God. Luther's *Small Catechism* expresses it this way:

> Our neighbor means everyone. We are to love all men as we love ourselves, not only our relatives, friends, and acquaintances, but strangers, enemies, and people of all nations and climes. We must be ready to do good to all who are in need of our help and kindness.[44]

Luther goes on to interpret the fifth commandment along two lines: what is forbidden and what is commanded. In terms of what is commanded, we should assist and comfort our neighbor in danger:

> We should warn him of danger; defend and rescue him, ward off danger from him; save him from worry and anxiety whenever we can. In want, we should aid the poor and destitute; minister to the sick; comfort the afflicted and distressed; give to organized charities;

orphanages, asylums, hospitals, rescue-work, etc.; give to missions in order to save souls.[45]

These acts of kindness, compassion, and mercy may be performed collectively through local churches as outreach and ministries to the community. Or they could be performed by individual Christians, alone, through secular agencies or other concerned citizens. But whether these acts are performed by churches or individual Christians, such neighborly love should not be confused with sharing the gospel. In other words, a church food giveaway is not the same thing as evangelism, and if a church does not have such a program, it has not failed in its calling as a church. The main ministry of the church, which is the Word and sacrament, should include equipping its members for ministry in the context both of the church and of the community. Here again the two-kingdom distinction is helpful. Failure to recognize the distinction is perhaps the means by which we get the rise of various social gospels. Christian service in the community could be a bridge that leads to evangelistic efforts, but they are not the same.

Let me conclude with a few observations.

1. The term "spirituality" is being used in a variety of ways today, few of which are consistent with biblical teaching or spirituality. Therefore the spiritual vitality of any church, whatever its ethnic character or denominational affiliation, must be measured in biblical terms and not according to the trends of the times.

2. Biblical spirituality consists in God working in us both to will and to do of his good pleasure through the instrumentality of his Word and Spirit. Therefore, hearing the Word preached and taught and personally studying the Word are inseparable from true spiritual formation. Our personal experiences and ecstasies are to be measured and governed by the Word. The work of the Spirit in our lives consists in him bringing us into union with the completed work of Christ and conforming us to his image. Both of these works are accomplished through the Word of God being brought to bear more and more on our thoughts, from which our actions flow. There is

no spirituality apart from knowledge and love of the truth of God's Word.

3. Although biblical spirituality consists in the work of the Spirit in the lives of believers, it is manifest in tangible deeds and actions. In Romans 12 the apostle Paul calls this our reasonable service. Far from being a private engagement or state of spiritual ecstasy for personal gratification, biblical spirituality is both horizontal and vertical as it relates to the two tables of the law: duties and affections toward God and others.

There is much being said and written regarding a new surge in spirituality among all races. Black churches have stepped on stage with other mega-churches, with our own star personalities, paraphernalia, and signs of success. But let us not mistake these things for genuine and biblical spirituality.

6

GRACE SO AMAZING
Experiencing the Doctrines of Grace

by ANTHONY J. CARTER

"A hero ain't nothing but a sandwich." So said Alice Childress in her book by the same title. I don't go in for too many oversized sandwiches, but I do know some men for whom no sandwich could do justice to their legacy. For my money, they are heroes of the highest sort, because they are heroes of faith. And one of my heroes of the Christian faith is John Newton.

John Newton

Unbeknownst to many, John Newton was not only a prolific hymn writer, but he was also an excellent pastor and theologian. Yet he is most known for his hymn writing. And though he wrote hundreds of hymns, including "How Sweet the Name of Jesus Sounds" and "Glorious Things of Thee Are Spoken," the one with which he is most associated is the seemingly canonized "Amazing Grace, How Sweet the Sound." John Newton is one of my heroes because, from the words of his signature hymn, I imagine him grieving over his sins

141

once grace appeared to him much in the same way I grieved over mine. I imagine him living the rest of his life amazed at the mercy of God toward such a sinner in the same way I stand amazed. John Newton's life after the appearance of grace is worthy of remembering, because his life before the appearance of mercy is so worthy of forgetting. So is mine.

John Newton grew up among sailors and seafaring men of eighteenth-century England. At the time such men were often the most crude, vitriolic, and insolent in English society. And to his own God-forsaking honor, and later to his God-glorying shame, John Newton was the most insolent of all. For John Newton was not just a sailor, but according to his own testimony, he was a sailor involved in the most insidious of all the seafaring businesses—slavery. He was a slave trader, and he was one of the best (or worst).

The slave trade in John Newton's day was a hideous occupation. And while it was quite lucrative and socially acceptable, it exacted a heavy price upon the souls and psyche of men. The trade, while accompanied by wealth and treasure, was also the source of every vile indiscretion one could imagine: murder, rape, disease, infanticide, stealing, lying, blasphemy, and so on. These vices were not the exception but the rule. And none of these sins escaped John Newton. That is, until he met the Savior.

John Newton had gained the reputation of being the most obstinate and vocal atheist at sea. However, one night in the midst of one of the worst storms he had ever encountered, he found himself totally helpless against the monstrous tempest. Without thought or understanding he cried out in the most desperate hour, "God have mercy on us!" Thinking he would be dead by dawn, when John Newton awoke the next morning to calm seas, his uncharacteristic cry for divine intervention troubled his soul. "What mercy is there for me?" he thought. Upon the Spirit pricking his soul, he discovered that not only was there abundant mercy for him, but there was also *amazing grace.*

One of John Newton's good friends was a man named William Cowper. Cowper and Newton combined to write the now famous *Olney Hymnal,* which contained some three hundred hymns. One of Cowper's better-known offerings begins, "God moves in a mysterious way/His wonders to perform." Indeed, Newton's life is a testimony to the mysterious, wondrous ways of God. That God would rise up and use John Newton is not only ironic but unmistakably providential.

The irony of God is all over the history of redemption. To look into history and see the men God used to accomplish various tasks is amazing. For example, when God decrees to choose a people upon whom he can set his affections, does he choose a God-fearing, worshipful man to be their patriarch? No, he chooses Abraham, a pagan idol worshipper to exemplify faithfulness to him. And whom would God use to lead the children of Israel out of Egypt? Surely he would not use an Egyptian noble. Yet God calls Moses, the one-time Prince of Egypt, to lead them out of Egypt. Also, when faced with a fast-growing and ever-expanding church during the first century, whom would God choose to inform the church of life and worship? Surely he would not choose a blasphemer and persecutor of the church. Yet indeed he chooses Paul, the grandest of blasphemers and persecutors of the church, to become the most prominent and the eminent apostle in the church. With such grand and imposing examples of God's often-ironic providence, it should not surprise us that God continues to operate in this unique way. In order to bring the scourge of the Atlantic slave trade to its knees and ultimately end it altogether in Great Britain, whom would God use? Surely not one who was himself a slave trader and a profiteer in human abuses. Yet God raised up the lowly slave-trading, infidelity-driven, Navy-constricted, impertinent, insolent, unbelieving John Newton.

John Newton lived and worked among the slaves, whom he abused and used for his sinful desires. Being one of the most proficient at this horrendous enterprise, he, more than anyone, knew the horror and damage the enterprise did to the soul and psyche of both the slave and the slave trader. He eloquently related the horror in the most graphic terms:

> But in general I know of no method of getting money, not even that of robbing for it upon the highway which has so direct a tendency to

efface the moral sense, to rob the heart of every gentle and humane disposition and to handle it, like steel, against all impressions of sensibility. . . [the Africans] are considered as a people to be robbed and spoiled with impunity. Every art is employed to deceive and wrong them. And he who has most address in this way, has most to boast of.[1]

And no one could boast of his efficiency more than John Newton.

Once God removed Newton from laboring on a slave ship, God not only cleansed Newton's heart, but he also cleared his mind and pricked his conscience. In 1764, God called Newton to the pastorate of a small parish church in Olney, England. From his pulpit ministry, he not only faithfully preached the Word to his parishioners, but he labored in word and deed to bring the "disagreeable service" of slavery to an end. He never shied away from sharing his testimony or from admitting how the experience became for him a thorn in the flesh.

> If my testimony should not be necessary or serviceable, yet perhaps I am bound in conscience to take shame to myself by a public confession, which however sincere comes too late to prevent or repair the misery and mischief to which I have formerly been accessory.
>
> I hope it will always be a subject of humiliating reflection to me, that I was once an active instrument in a business at which my heart now shudders.[2]

Under the direct influence of John Newton, the grand English statesman, William Wilberforce, was able to push legislation through Parliament abolishing the slave trade in England in February of 1807 and the entire disagreeable and regretful institution in July of 1833. John Newton's legacy in the church was that his life of slave trading led to the abolishment of the slave trade, and then he gave to the sons and daughters of those slaves he had traded the song that would inform their struggle for freedom from oppression and assurance in God—"Amazing Grace."

John Newton wrote "Amazing Grace," the most beloved hymn

in the African-American church (and in all English-speaking Christianity), after reflecting upon his life before grace appeared to him and wrought the efficacious work of redemption in his life:

Amazing grace, how sweet the sound
That saved a wretch like me!
I once was lost but now I'm found,
Was blind, but now I see.

'Twas grace that taught my heart to fear,
And grace my fears relieved;
How precious did that grace appear,
The hour I first believed!

Thro' many dangers, toils, and snares,
I have already come;
'Tis grace has brought me safe thus far,
And grace will lead me home.

Newton's words, though reflective of his personal experience, crossed experiential lives to speak and express the experiences of even the sons and daughters of oppression in America. As Steve Turner, the author of the acclaimed *Amazing Grace: The Story of America's Most Beloved Song*, writes:

The first slaves to sing "Amazing Grace" wouldn't have known the story of John Newton and would therefore have been unaware of the irony involved in expressing their hopes through the words of a man who had helped capture their ancestors in Africa and transport them across the Atlantic. By the time of emancipation there would have been more than fourteen thousand direct descendants of the slaves brought to Charleston on the *Brownlow* and around forty thousand descendants of those brought to the Caribbean on the two ships Newton commanded.[3]

Ever since their first exposure to John Newton's hymn, African-American Christians have never failed to sing it with a passion and a uniqueness that make it their own. American slaves found in his words a kindred spirit of hope for a brighter day. They found in his verse the expressions of souls longing for heaven, knowing that they deserved far less. No matter how dark the hour or how troubled the soul, they could sing of God's amazing grace, and immediately the clouds would be lifted and the disquieted soul would be refreshed. The grace of which John Newton wrote and slaves sung was a grace that extended to both the slave and the slave trader. It reminded them and it reminds us that at the cross all ground is flat and we all stand in need. How amazing!

Lemuel Haynes

While our God was at work with one hand in England fashioning a hero we all can praise God for, he was simultaneously preparing heroes (not sandwiches) of a darker hue through whom he would demonstrate his amazing grace on the other side of the Atlantic. One of these grace-endowed, Spirit-guided men was Lemuel Haynes.

Lemuel Haynes was born in West Hartford, Connecticut, on July 18, 1753, eleven years prior to John Newton's assuming the pastorate of the Church of Olney. Haynes was the illegitimate child of a white woman and a black man. His mother, whom Lemuel Haynes's earliest biographer, Timothy Mather Cooley, refers to as "a woman of respectable New England ancestry,"[4] abandoned the young boy at birth because as a newborn he "so resembled his father . . . that the woman decided to leave her infant in the care of others,"[5] rather than suffer the social ramifications of having a mulatto baby. Shortly after birth, Haynes was given to Mr. and Mrs. David Rose, a pious and God-fearing couple from Durham, Connecticut. Here Haynes found a home; he was accepted by the Rose family as one of its own.

As a young boy, Haynes gravitated to the pious nature of the Rose family and quickly excelled in the exercise of religion. He was allowed to attend the district school, but responsibilities with the family farm took away nearly every opportunity for formal training. Yet far more critical in his development was the religious instruction he caught from the Rose family as they observed Sabbath, daily prayers, and religious instruction. Accordingly, "Haynes was a determined self-taught student who poured over Scripture until he could repeat from memory most of the texts dealing with the *doctrines of grace,* a feat that impressed almost everyone who later heard him in the pulpit."[6] Haynes's pulpit ministry was remarkable.

Following his discharge from the Continental Army during the Revolutionary War, Haynes returned home and began studying theology (when not working in the fields). Soon others recognized his gifts and calling for the ministry. The impetus for this recognition occurred quite unexpectedly one Saturday night during family worship:

> Haynes was usually designated to read the text chosen for study. On this occasion he substituted a sermon he had written himself, without revealing its authorship. Those present were truly impressed when Haynes admitted that it was not a work of Watts, Whitefield, Doddridge, or Davie but, in fact his own composition. He began to gain a reputation as one raised up of God for more than common usefulness, and was urged to enter the ministry.[7]

In November 1785 Lemuel Haynes became the first black American to be ordained by any religious organization in America. Following three years of itinerant ministry, Haynes was called to Rutland, Vermont, where he assumed the pastorate of the Congregational church. He was the first black American to receive a call to pastor an all-white congregation. Here he faithfully labored for thirty years as pastor and preacher. His sermons were both intellectually stimulating and engagingly presented. Following the example of the great evangelical stalwarts of his day, Haynes preached the glorious doctrines of grace that so defined the ministry of men like George Whitefield and Jonathan Edwards. He believed that the sovereign grace of God would bring revival, therefore his preaching proclaimed and promoted such revivals of religion. In fact, "Haynes' sermons themselves best illustrate his evangelical Calvinistic theological stance, consistently indicating an unwavering belief in predestination and personal election."[8]

Haynes was quick to see the hand of Providence in all things. He never seemed to miss the opportunity to describe and even relish in the glorious Providence that guided and directed all events. After he was unexpectedly rescued from sure drowning by a friend, he frequently used this harrowing affair as an illustration and fodder for discussing "the special and merciful care of Divine providence towards himself in that dangerous season of life."[9] In fact, it was his understanding of God's sovereign mercy and providence that drew him to John Newton. In the writings of Newton, Haynes found a kindred spirit. Like Newton, Haynes's life was wrought with near-death experiences, experiences Haynes always "remembered and mentioned with much gratitude."[10] So familiar was he with the providence and grace of which Newton wrote that he often expressed his familiarity by quoting a favorite passage from the writings of John Newton: "Did I not believe in the particular providence of God, I should not dare step my foot out of doors."[11]

Lemuel Haynes, like John Newton before him, and countless other Christian faithful before them, loved the grace of God and sought to live upon it. To them it was not a doctrine that belonged to the ethereal realm, but rather was the source of the Christian's strength and the hope of eternity. To both men, in a word—grace was *amazing*.

Doctrines of Grace

What makes grace so amazing? What is it about grace that caused John Newton to marvel at it and to write of its wonder in verse? What is it about grace that caused Lemuel Haynes to live so close to it and proclaim it so boldly? It is that grace is full of the purposes of God in the life of his people. Grace is the motive and means by which God draws near to his people that they may in turn draw near to him. Grace is a doctrine; in fact, it is a series of doctrines that has both theoretical and practical importance for the church. GRACE is:[12]

God's Sovereign Election (also known as unconditional election). That God is sovereign is an undeniable truth taught throughout the Bible. He is sovereign over all things, from the rain that falls on the earth (Amos 4:7) to the kings who reign on the earth (Prov. 21:1).

There is no place to which his sovereignty does not reach. This includes the election of human beings unto salvation. The Bible is clear that, as Christians, God chose us in him before the foundation of the world to be holy and without blame before him in love, having predestined us to adoption as sons by Jesus Christ to himself, according to the good pleasure of his will (Eph. 1:4–5). We are elect by God not because we ran so hard or willed so strongly, but because he is merciful (Rom. 9:15–16). The Bible that says that God is sovereign over the weather is the Bible that says God is sovereign in election.

Radical Depravity (also known as total depravity or human inability). There is no questioning that the Bible represents humans as being in rebellion and even at war with God. This warfare is the manifestation of sin, which, when it entered by Adam (Rom. 5:12), pervaded our entire existence. So now all people are reckoned, apart from Christ, as being spiritually dead in trespasses and sins (Eph. 2:1). Apart from Christ we are perpetually engaging in the lust of our flesh, fulfilling the desires of the flesh and of the mind, and are by nature (that is, birth) children of wrath (Eph. 2:3). The grip of sin on the natural human being makes him not only unwilling but even unable to submit to the will and ways of God or to please God by good deeds (Rom. 8:7–8). This is to say that humans are morally corrupt, even radically depraved. Or as the Bible says, "sold under sin" (Rom 7:14).

Accomplished Redemption (also known as limited atonement or particular redemption). The coming of Christ into the world had an intentional divine purpose. He came to save sinners from their sin. This was the purpose of Christ on the earth because it was the purpose of God from all eternity. The Bible speaks of Christ's death on the cross as being intentional and designed. Christ saved his people from their sins (Matt. 1:21). He was the shepherd who laid down his life for his sheep (John 10:14–15). He gave his life for the church (Eph. 5:25). His people, his sheep, and the church are just synonyms for the elect whom God had chosen for redemption before the foundations of the world (Eph. 1:4–5). We are not to think of Christ making salvation *possible* for his sheep, his people, or the church. We are to understand that the redemption he came to bring to the elect is the redemption he *accomplished*, once and for all for his people (Heb. 7:27).

Called Effectually (also known as irresistible grace or efficacious grace). This aspect of God's salvific work speaks to the efficacious nature of God's salvation. All those whom God has appointed unto salvation (Acts 13:48) not only receive the outward call of the gospel (all who hear the preached Word thus receive this external calling), but will also inevitably receive the inward call of the Holy Spirit (Acts 16:14; Rom. 8:30; 2 Tim. 1:9). By this work of the Holy Spirit they are drawn unto him in salvation (Matt. 11:25–27; John 6:37, 44–45; 10:4, 14–16). This is the regenerating work of God in the heart of a sinner, which is not thwarted or compromised. For if God determines to save someone, who can deter his purpose? In this we can say that his grace, when supernaturally imparted, while it may be resisted, overcomes human resistance.

Endurance of the Saints (also known as perseverance or preservation of the saints). The final point is a fitting culmination of the previous points. God preserves those who come to faith through the efficacious work of God in redemption until their final redemption is accomplished (Eph. 4:30; Col. 3:3–4; 2 Tim. 1:12). Those whom God has called and justified by his grace will be glorified to his glory (Rom. 8:29–30, 35–40), and none of those whom he has ordained unto salvation shall be lost (John 6:35–40; 10:27–30). Thus, the unconquerable keeping power of God causes his saints to endure, even persevere, until the end. They will endure in grace, because he who has begun a good work in them will complete it until the day of Jesus Christ (Phil. 1:6). The saved endure because they are secure; they are kept by the power of God through faith for salvation ready to be revealed in the last time (1 Pet. 1:5). In other words, we are not elected by God only to be rejected by God. We, who are elected in eternity, are protected in time.

For centuries these grand doctrines have shaped the understanding and teaching of the Protestant church. And while the predominantly black church in America has been overwhelmingly Protestant, it has failed to see that at the root of Protestantism are these glorious doctrines. Subsequently, it is safe to say that if you belong to a Protestant church today, somewhere along your church's historical timeline it accepted, rejected, or neglected the doctrines of grace. Therefore, to understand your church and your faith is to understand these truths and how they have developed in your church's understanding.

If you are Protestant today, then you trace your Christian roots to the Protestant Reformation of the sixteenth century. The doctrines of grace defined the Reformation and gave to its adherents a systemization of the biblical truths of salvation, which historical Christianity has held so dear. And though the doctrines are often referred to as the Five Points of Calvinism (see endnote 12), they were not invented by John Calvin. Two contemporary pastors and theologians make this point clear:

> Although these doctrines constitute the purest expression of Calvinism, Calvin did not invent them, nor were they characteristic of his thought alone during the Reformation period. These truths are contained in the Old Testament Psalms. They were taught by Jesus, even to his enemies, as recorded in John 6 and 10 and elsewhere. The apostle Paul confirmed them in his letters to the Romans, the Ephesians, and others. Saint Augustine argued for the same truths over against the denials of Pelagius. Martin Luther was in many ways a Calvinist (as, in many respects, Calvin was a Lutheran). So were Ulrich Zwingli and William Tyndale. For this reason, it is perhaps more accurate to describe this theology as "Reformational" rather than "Calvinistic." The Puritans were Reformed theologians, too, and it was through their teaching that England and Scotland experienced some of the greatest and most pervasive national revivals the world has ever seen. Among these Puritans were the heirs of the Scottish Reformer John Knox: Thomas Cartwright, Richard Sibbes, John Owen, John Bunyan, Matthew Henry, Thomas Boston, and many others. In America many thousands were influenced by Jonathan Edwards, Cotton Mather, and George Whitefield, all of whom were Calvinists.
>
> In more recent times the modern missionary movement received its direction and initial impetus from those in the Reformed tradition. The list of these pioneers includes such great missionaries as

William Carey, John Ryland, Henry Martyn, Robert Moffat, David Livingstone, John G. Paton, and John R. Mott. For all of these men, the doctrines of grace were not merely an appendage to Christian thought; rather, these were the central doctrines that fueled their evangelistic fires and gave form to their preaching of the gospel.[13]

You may or may not be familiar with many of the above-mentioned names, but any study of the history of Protestant Christianity will be saturated with these men and others whose lives of faith were a testimony to the biblical convictions of the doctrines of grace and the life of faith these doctrines inevitably produce. Yet, the importance of those doctrines is demonstrated not only by the lives of those who espoused them (a Who's Who of Protestant Christianity), but also by how these doctrines can and should inform our understanding of ourselves today. This is particularly true in the predominantly African-American church, of which I am a proud son.

In *On Being Black and Reformed*, I argued for an understanding of the African-American Christian experience from the historical and biblical Reformed perspective. Only in understanding the biblical doctrines of the sovereignty of God, the sinfulness of humans, and the sufficiency of Christ do we get an adequate and God-glorifying perspective on history in general and on the African-American experience in particular. In this follow-up volume, we have argued for the essentialness of Reformed theology for the evangelical church at large and the predominantly African-American church in particular. We also suggest that this begins with an investigation and appropriation of the doctrines of grace.

While many may suggest that the doctrines of grace are foreign to the African-American Christian experience, we want to suggest that they are inherent in understanding any of God's salvific dealing with his people. Definitively, God's relationship with us is a manifestation of and based in his sovereign and amazing grace. And nothing so accurately and gloriously demonstrates his grace than do the doctrines of grace. We can say this just as Newton said it.

Why is grace so amazing? First, grace is amazing because we are amazing sinners. To contemplate the depths of one's own sinfulness is to agree with John Newton's self assessment in decrying himself as "wretched." For Newton, the exaltation of sin was not to sin's credit but was to the greater exaltation of the Savior. Second, grace is amazing because we have an amazing Savior. Sin so great demands a sacrifice greater still. The witness of John Newton in verse is so powerful and popular because in our hearts it rings true and reminds us of our only hope in life and death—*the amazing grace of God.*

Sermon Preparation

The key to faithful preaching is preparation. Remember, the Bible is not a newspaper. Each passage of Scripture must be interpreted within its immediate context and the context of the overall message of Scripture. Therefore, preparation is key. There is no canonical method for sermon preparation; each preacher tends to develop his own. However, the basic approach tends to be the same, with only the emphases being different. Below are the basic steps in my own sermon preparation. Hopefully it will encourage a similar preparation for others.

1. **Read the Text**. I read the passage several times, making sure to read the text in its context. I read the text in several translations (both literal and loose). I read the text in the original language (particularly in New Testament Greek). My Old Testament Hebrew reading ability is, for the most part, nonexistent. I rely heavily upon Hebrew language help resources.

2. **Analyze the Text**. I go over the passage, making note of key and recurring words, key phrases, and important themes. I do lexical work on key words and identify helpful important nuances of the

grammar not easily seen in the English Bible. There are a multitude of Bible linguistic programs, such as *BibleWorks,* which offer invaluable exegetical resources at the touch of your mouse or keypad. Don't be ashamed to use them. God has gifted the church with brilliant men and women who have written extensive books and computer programs for helping us understand both New Testament Greek and Old Testament Hebrew. Don't hesitate to use them. It is more important that we get it right than we do all the leg work ourselves.

3. **Develop an Outline.** Here I identify the major theme or idea of the passage and develop an outline featuring major and minor points I may want to bring out. Introduction and conclusion are usually developed about this time—they are key for me.

4. **Study Cross References**. As I develop major points, I find supportive Scriptures for each point. This also is a good time to make note of illustrations, though illustrations generally come throughout the process.

5. **Read Commentaries**. I begin checking my work against expositors who have looked intently at the passage before me. I make sure my major points coincide with theirs. If there is a conflict, *I do not ignore it.* I seek to resolve any conflicts so that I am not the first to make a given point. I also enjoy reading a wide range of commentaries from old to new, conservative to liberal, devotional to technical.

6. **Listen to Others**. This is a step that is more available in our day than in previous times. The Internet affords us a wealth of preaching and sermon resources. I try to listen to a couple of sermons on the same passage or subject. This is another way of checking my content and being encouraged by others. I find this not only helpful, but inspirational as well.

7. **Write the Outline (Final Draft).** This is the draft I will take into the pulpit. I usually preach from an outline, with which I am very

familiar.[1] For a Sunday sermon this outline will usually be completed on Friday and Saturday.

8. **Meditate**. This is the final step in my sermon preparation. I spend time—at different times—meditating upon the sermon and praying over its various aspects. This is a time when I envision myself preaching the sermon and how I will emphasize certain points. It is also when I am able to ask God specifically to empower certain aspects of the delivery. This is when I become so familiar with the sermon that I will not need to rely too heavily on my notes.

SAMPLE SERMON OUTLINE

What's It All about, Charlie Brown?

Luke 2:8–14

I. **Introduction**. It's been forty years since a *Charlie Brown Christmas* debuted on network television, instantly becoming one of the most popular holiday specials of all time.

II. **What Is It All About? It's about Peace, Charlie Brown**. When Linus walked to the center of the stage to give that now famous recital of Luke 2:8–14, he was answering Charlie Brown's question with the most profound and yet simplest answers of all. He declared to Charlie Brown and all those gathered that day that Christmas is about peace. For when the angel appeared to the shepherds, just outside of the small town of Bethlehem, he essentially gave and demonstrated a message of good news, of great joy, of peace.

This is the message of Christmas. This is the message not only to Charlie Brown, but to you and me. Peace has come into the world. Peace has come down. Peace has been preached to us. Peace has been brought near. It is a great peace. It is a glorious peace. It is a marvelous, an *in excelsis Deo* peace. But it is not just a peace given to the shepherds out in the Judean hillside; it is a peace that is given to us this day. It is a peace that is given to each of us if we would so celebrate the true meaning of Christmas.

But what is this peace? What makes it so incomparable? Why should I know it? Because there is a peace that passes all understanding. There is a blessed, holy quietness. There is a calm assurance that all is well. There is a peace of mind that comes from knowing and living upon Jesus. What manner of peace is this, Charlie Brown? There are four elements to this peace, to this blessed assurance.

A. **A Peace That Conquers Fear (v. 9–10).** When the angel of God appeared to the shepherds, the shepherds were gripped with fear; they were sorely afraid.

1. They feared the messenger. And well they should have. It appears that angels could be intimidating beings. According to the biblical record, angels often inspired awe and fear in human beings (1 Chron. 21:30; Matt. 28:5; Luke 1:13; Luke 1:30).

2. They feared the manifestation. If the angel was intimidating and awe-inspiring, the glory of God—the manifest brilliance of his presence—was even more so.

3. But the message of the angels this day is not a message of terror; it is not a message of judgment or destruction. It is a message of peace. Therefore, *do not be afraid* of the messenger or the manifestation.

4. Nevertheless, on every turn we are afraid. We experience fear. Despite our Lord's consistent admonitions not to be afraid, we still are incessantly fearful. We are afraid because we lack peace.

5. A lack of peace is often the manifestation of misplaced fear.
    a. Too often we fear those things we should not and fear not those things we should.
    b. We fear men and women.
    c. We lack a fear of God and his Word.

d. Jesus tells us where our fears should be rightly directed (Luke 12:5).

B. **A Peace That Carries Good News (v. 10)**. The angel of God not only tells the shepherds not to fear, but also tells them why they must not fear.

1. The angel of God has good news. The message of the angel is a message that is "good" and it is "news."

2. The good news will bring great joy. This is the message that conquers fear, because it replaces fear with "great joy." It is "joy inexpressible," as Peter puts it in 1 Peter 1:8.

3. The *euaggelizo*. The angels come with a message of "good news," or in some of your translations it says "good tidings." The word in the Greek is *euaggelizo*, from which we get the word "evangelize." This is the first mention of this word, but from this point in the Bible on it will be the word used to announce the preaching of the gospel, the proclaiming of the gospel of the kingdom, the gospel of peace.

   In Romans 10:14–15 Paul asks the rhetorical question concerning salvation, "How then will they call on him in whom they have not believed? And how are they to believe in him of whom they have never heard? And how are they to hear without someone preaching? And how are they to preach unless they are sent? As it is written, '*How beautiful are the feet of those who preach the good news!*'"

4. But the good news is only good if the bad news is really bad. And this is really why the good news is so good: the bad news is *really* bad. Unfortunately, in our day we have lost the terror of the bad news, and therefore we rarely know the great joy of the good news. May I remind you of the bad news?

   The bad news had been around for a long time. It is the awesome and sobering truth that sinful human beings are at war with God. Ever since the fall of Adam and Eve, humans have been alienated from God; we have been out of it with God. God was angry with Adam and Eve's sin. God was angry with Adam and Eve.

The bad news is that God is angry at our sin. God is angry at sinners. Every day his anger is kindled against them; every day the sinner heaps coal upon the burning wrath of God. Everyday he stokes the fire of God's righteous wrath against sin.

Every day that sinners exist in this world without experiencing the full judgment of God's holiness is a moment of unmitigated mercy and grace. The bad news is that sinners are enemies of God; they are in a battle with God that they cannot win, and yet they go on fighting every day. The bad news is that God destroys his enemies, and when he decides to do so, he destroys them swiftly and totally. The bad news is that the war continues and there is no cease fire, there is no peace—until God declares peace. There is no peace until God sends the message of peace.

There is no peace until the angel comes to the shepherds and says, "I have a message for all peoples: you need study war no more." The peace that was lost in the garden of Eden has been born in Bethlehem. The peace Adam and Eve forfeited in their rebellion is lying in a stable in a manger in Bethlehem.

Joy to the world, our peace has come. Let earth receive her King!

C. **A Peace That Confirms Promises (v. 11–12)**. The coming of the Messiah is good news to the shepherds and to you and me. But it was not new news to the plan of God.

1. This peace was signaled in the Old Testament. For years people have been trying to count the number of prophecies in the Old Testament that were fulfilled in the coming of Christ. By conservative estimates there may be some three hundred prophesies concerning the first coming of Christ. Many were fulfilled in his birth:
   a. Isaiah 7:14: he would be born of a virgin girl. See Luke 1:27.
   b. Isaiah 7:14: he would be called Immanuel. See Matthew 1:23.
   c. Isaiah 9:7: he would sit upon the throne of David. See Luke 1:32–33.
   d. Micah 5:2: his place of birth would be Bethlehem, the city of David. See Luke 2:11.

   The movie the *Ten Commandments* has Yul Brenner playing Ramses, the Egyptian Pharaoh. One of his more famous lines is, "So let it be written; so let it be done."
   Isaiah 40:8 reminds us that, "the grass withers, and the flowers fade but the word of our God will stand forever." Or in other words, "So let it be written, so let it be done."

2. This peace is solidified in the New Testament. For the prophecy to all was that the Messiah would be born in Bethlehem, in the city of David. Yet there is another sign; there is another promise associated with this peace. There is given to the shepherds another sure word of prophecy (v. 12).
   a. How many babies were born in Bethlehem that night? We could venture a guess and say quite a few.
   b. How many babies were born in Bethlehem and wrapped in swaddling clothes? We again could venture a guess and say quite a few.

    c. But how many babies were born in Bethlehem, wrapped in swaddling clothes, and lying in a manger? How many newborns were delivered in a stable and placed in a feeding trough? I would venture a guess and say, *only one.*

D. A Peace That Concludes in Praise (v. 14). The message of peace from the angel concludes with the glorious note of the angelic host raising their voices in praise.

    1. Once awestruck with fear, the shepherds are now overwhelmed with joy. And what is the response of anyone who has seen the glory and power of God? It is worship. Indeed, a heart and mind filled with peace, with a confident assurance that God's Word is true, and with the blessed quietness of knowing he will do what he said he will do is a life prepared to praise. In other words, when fear gives way to joy, the result is praise.

    2. We can only imagine the fear that must have gripped the shepherds' hearts as the angel of God appeared to them. We can only imagine the fear that must have attended them as they saw the manifest glory of God shine all around them. Oh, but what joy must have filled their hearts when they heard the angels singing!

    3. We are a singing people. We sing because we are happy. We sing because we are free. We sing because we know God is good. We sing all year long. But the best songs are at Christmastime. And well it should be. You see, at the crucifixion of Jesus there was no singing. Even at his resurrection, we read of no songs being sung. But when it was time for him to be born, there were songs aplenty.

        a. Mary in her Magnificat in Luke 1:46–47: "My soul magnifies the Lord, and my spirit rejoices in God my Savior."

b. Zechariah in the Benedictus in Luke 1:68–69: "Blessed be the Lord God of Israel, for he has visited and redeemed his people and has raised up a horn of salvation for us in the house of his servant David. . . ."

c. And then we have the angels: "Glory to God in the highest, and on earth peace among those with whom he is pleased!"

III. **What's It All about Charlie Brown?** It's about peace, Charlie Brown! And if it's about peace, then it's about Jesus.

A. Do you have this peace this year? You can't look to the president for it. You see he can't bring it. Arresting terrorists or tracking down and killing Osama Bin Laden won't bring peace.

B. You can't find it on the rack at Neiman Marcus. You can't locate it under the blue light at Kmart, or among the falling prices of Wal-Mart.

C. Acts 10:36 reminds us that this peace comes only through Jesus Christ the Lord. And, even more specific, Colossians 1:20 tells us that this peace comes only through the blood of his cross.

Sample Orders of Worship

Order of Worship for Southwest Christian Fellowship, Atlanta

Call to Worship/Invocation

Responsive Reading :   Psalm 33:1–6

Leader:	Rejoice in the Lord, O you righteous! *For* praise from the upright is beautiful.
Congregation:	Praise the Lord with the harp; Make melody to Him with an instrument of ten strings.
Leader:	Sing to Him a new song; Play skillfully with a shout of joy.
Congregation:	For the word of the Lord *is* right, And all His work *is done* in truth.
Leader:	He loves righteousness and justice; The earth is full of the goodness of the Lord.
Together:	By the word of the Lord the heavens were made, And all the host of them by the breath of His mouth.

Congregational Hymn
"All Hail the Power of Jesus Name"

Communion Meditation / Observance
Pastor Anthony Carter

Songs of Praise
SCF Praise Team and Congregation

Pastoral Greeting and Prayer
Pastor Robert Benson

The Lord's Prayer (unison)
Our Father who art in heaven, Hallowed be thy name.
Thy kingdom come. Thy will be done in earth, as *it is* in heaven.
Give us this day our daily bread.
And forgive us our debts, as we forgive our debtors.
And lead us not into temptation, but deliver us from evil:
For thine is the kingdom, and the power, and the glory, for ever.
Amen.

Prayer Meditation
"Kyrie Eleison" (Lord Have Mercy)

Ministry in Giving
Pastor Carter

Announcements
Pastor Carter

Scripture Reading
Luke 17:20-37
Pastor Carter

Ministry in Music
Southwest Christian Fellowship Choir

Ministry of the Word:
Looking for the Kingdom
Pastor Benson

Benediction
"Doxology"

Order of Worship for All Saints Redeemer Church, Stone Mountain, GA:

The Call to Worship

Invocation
Pastor Michael Leach

The Responsive Reading
Reverend Roderick Bell

Leader:	Come up to me on the mountain and wait there, that I may give you the tablets of stone,
Congregation:	Come and see what God has done: he is awesome in his deeds toward the children of man.
Leader:	Come now, let us reason together, says the LORD:
Congregation:	Come, my people, enter your chambers, and shut your doors behind you; hide yourselves for a little while until the fury has passed by.
Leader:	Come, and hear what the word is that comes from the LORD.
Congregation:	Come to me, all who labor and are heavy laden, and I will give you rest.
Leader:	Tell those who are invited, everything is ready. Come to the wedding feast.
Congregation:	The Spirit and the Bride say, "Come." And let the one who hears say, "Come."

Leader: And let the one who is thirsty come; let the one who desires take the water of life without price.

Congregation: O house of Jacob, come, let us walk in the light of the LORD.

TOGETHER: Come, you who are blessed by my Father, inherit the kingdom prepared for you from the foundation of the world.

Songs of Affirmation: "Stand Up, and Bless the Lord"; "The King of Love My Shepherd Is"

Corporate Prayer
Reverend Roderick
> Prayer of Adoration
> Prayer of Confession
> Assurance of Pardon

Worship in Song
Psalm 126. Sung to the Tune of "My Faith Looks up to Thee"

The Ministry of Giving
The Offertory and Prayer of Thanksgiving

The Ministry of the Word

The Reading of the Law	Deuteronomy 5:7, 8, 11, 12, 16–18, 20, 21; 6:1, 2
The Reading of the Gospel	Romans 3:21–26

The Westminster Larger Catechism, # 80

> **Q:** Can true believers be infallibly assured that they are in the estate of grace, and that they shall persevere therein unto salvation?

> **A.** Such as truly believe in Christ, and endeavor to walk in all good conscience before him, may, without extraordinary revelation, by faith grounded upon the truth of God's promises, and by the Spirit enabling them to discern in themselves those graces

to which the promises of life are made, and bearing witness with their spirits that they are the children of God, be infallibly assured that they are in the estate of grace, and shall persevere therein unto salvation.

The Word in Song (See Screen)

The Preaching of the Word
Pastor Leach
   Text: Isaiah 55:1–3
   Title: The Ultimate Happy Meal

The Celebration of the Lord's Supper

The Hymn of Parting: "How Firm a Foundation"

The Benediction

The Doxology

NOTES

Chapter 1: Experiencing the Truth: An Introduction

1. Leonard Smith, "Did a Woman Choose Your Church?" *Gospel Today*, January 2006, 52.

2. Ibid., 54. The author of the article admits, "This is by no means an exhaustive list; it is only the beginning of a lengthy litany of wrong reasons, many of which are primary among men's justification for attending the churches they do."

3. Ibid., 55.

4. Anthony J. Carter, *On Being Black and Reformed* (Phillipsburg, NJ: P&R, 2003).

5. George Barna and Harry R. Jackson Jr., *High Impact African-American Churches: Leadership Concepts from Some of Today's Most Effective Churches* (Ventura, CA: Regal Books, 2004), 23.

6. Ibid., 28.

7. John W. Fountain, "No Place for Me," *Washington Post*, July 17, 2005, http://www.washingtonpost.com/wp-dyn/content/article/2005/07/15/AR2005071502194.html?referrer=emailarticle.

8. Ibid.

9. Ken Jones, "The Dangers of Not Guarding Your Hermeneutic," African-American Pastors Conference, Glendale Baptist Church, Miami, 2005.

10. Martyn Lloyd-Jones, *Justification by Faith: Historical Analysis*, Westminster Theological Seminary tape series.

11. Quoted in Nathan O. Hatch, *The Democratization of American Christianity* (New Haven, CT: Yale University Press, 1989), 102.

12. Wilhelmus à Brakel, *The Christian's Reasonable Service* (Grand Rapids, MI: Reformation Heritage Books, 1992), 2:132.

13. Ibid., 1:xx.

14. Ibid., 1:cxv.

Chapter 2: Biblical Theology: Experiencing the Truth about God

1. Quoted from the Internet Movie Database, http://www.imdb.com/name/nm0000669/bio/.

2. We are woefully regressing from the profound achievements and re-affirmations of the sixteenth-century Reformation, a restorative movement whose overall slogan was *post tenebras, lux,* "after darkness, light." That is to say, after centuries of darkness imposed by the obscurantism of Roman Catholic medievalism, the Reformation sought to restore the pure light of the gospel of Jesus Christ in the church and the world.

3. Taken from Dale P. Andrews, *Practical Theology for Black Churches* (London: Westminster John Knox, 2002), 1. George Barna and Harry R. Jackson Jr. used this quote in their celebrated work, *High Impact African-American Churches* (Ventura, Ca.: Regal Books, 2004), 79. Emphasis added.

4. Barna and Jackson, *High Impact African-American Churches.* According to these writers, high-impact Black churches are mega-churches. They mention that these were of a higher percentage than their Hispanic and White counterparts, with at least one dozen exceeding Willow Creek and Saddleback, two of the larger Anglo mega-churches, in weekly attendance by at least two thousand persons (p. 28). Further, they record that these huge Black churches "are poised to grow unusually large" (p. 68). Indeed many of them already have. The number of Black mega-churches with at least fifteen thousand members "is perhaps one of the best-kept secrets in the ministry world."

5. Richard Lints, *The Fabric of Theology: A Prolegomenon to Evangelical Theology* (Grand Rapids, MI: Eerdmans, 1993), 57.

6. Barna and Jackson, *High Impact African-American Churches,* 72–74.

7. Ibid., 40–41. Emphasis added.

8. Our Lord Jesus Christ himself defines the life that he gives to his disciples—eternal life—as consisting of the true knowledge of the Triune God: "And this is eternal life, that they know you the only true God, and Jesus Christ whom you have sent" (John 17:3).

9. In Lints, *Fabric of Theology,* 29. Lints attributes this quote to Peter Berger, *The Noise of Solemn Assemblies* (Garden City, NY: Doubleday, 1961), 124.

10. Lints, *Fabric of Theology,* 93.

11. Geerhardus Vos, *Biblical Theology: Old and New Testaments* (Edinburgh: Banner of Truth, 1994), 3.

12. Ibid., 4.

13. *The Westminster Confession of Faith,* 7:1.

14. In a real sense, the opening words of the biblical canon, "In the beginning, God created the heavens and the earth" (Gen. 1:1), strongly intimate the eternal division between Creator and creation. This opening salvo of eternal truth establishes the foundation for God's unmatchable uniqueness and immediately stifles any presuming notions of pantheism and any ambitious claims to apotheosis.

15. Richard B. Gaffin Jr., ed. *Redemptive History and Biblical Interpretation: The Shorter Writings of Geerhardus Vos* (Phillipsburg, NJ: P&R, 1980), 4.

16. These principles find clearer expression in what is called the covenant of works, which may be defined as an agreement instigated by the sovereign goodness and love of God as Creator and Adam as creature, for Adam's fullest blessing and for God's glory. Its very terminology signifies that the first Adam's obedience to God was the basis of his relationship and continued fellowship with his Creator. In this covenant, Adam did not act alone but as the God-appointed head and representative of all mankind to whom would be imputed divine blessings for his obedience or divine curses for his disobedience. The headship, representative, and obedience motifs are critical to our understanding the obedient, faithful role of Jesus Christ, the second Adam, in securing redemption for the elect of God. See Romans 5:12–21.

17. Vos, *Biblical Theology*, 4.

18. Ibid. Emphasis added.

19. Gaffin, *Redemptive History and Biblical Interpretation*, 4, 5.

20. *WCF,* 7:3.

21. Vos lays out these four characteristics in *Biblical Theology*, 5.

22. Gaffin, *Redemptive History and Biblical Interpretation*, 7.

23. Vos, *Biblical Theology*, 5–6.

24. Ibid., 9.

25. Ibid., 6–7.

26. Graeme Goldsworthy, "Gospel and Kingdom" in *The Goldsworthy Trilogy*, (Carlisle, UK: Paternoster, 2006), Seventh Impression, 104.

27. Adapted from O. Palmer Robertson in his June 26, 2002, interview on biblical theology with Mark Dever, accessed at http://resources.christianity.com/details/mrki/20020626/AB38BE35-17BC-465B-A0B9-537B27177BAB.aspx/. Dr. Warren Gage also develops this point in his short but salient work, *The Gospel of Genesis: Studies in Protology and Eschatology* (Winona Lake, Indiana: Carpenter Books, 1982), 7–8. From these opening pages, Gage successfully argues that the organic unity of Scripture, established by God's telic design in the creation narrative, is constantly reaffirmed throughout Scripture. Indeed, Gage states that the very words "in the beginning," an expression setting forth the beginning of history, strongly imply a historical, unfolding ending marked by the eschatological phrase, the "ending of days." Indeed, Scripture is characterized by an eschatological scheme "comprehending its entire scope." This diachronous way of viewing redemptive history informs us of an undeniable principle that biblical eschatology (the study of last things) is contained in and is based upon biblical protology (the study of first things). Why should this not be the case when Scripture is the revelation of the One who writes history from the beginning to the end? Further, why should it not be when Scripture reflects the very character of the One who is at the same time the beginning and the end, the Alpha and the Omega, the first and the last, the Son of David, as well as the root of Jesse?

28. Vos, *Biblical Theology*, 8.

29. Edmund P. Clowney, *Preaching and Biblical Theology* (Grand Rapids, MI: Eerdmans, 1961), 79.

30. Geerhardus Vos, "The Nature and Aims of Biblical Theology," http://www.kerux.com/documents/keruxv14n1a1.htm.

31. *The Westminster Larger Catechism*, question 12.

32. *WCF*, 2:2.

33. Adapted from Gene Edward Veith, "Confusing Faith and Fiction" *Tabletalk*, 30, no. 5 (May, 2006), 63.

34. Clowney, *Preaching and Biblical Theology*, 78–79.

35. Ibid., 88.

36. This necessarily raises the question, what happens to those whom God has not chosen unto eternal life? Does he equally and effectually work and create sin and disobedience in them to bring them to eternal damnation as he positively intervenes in the lives of his elect to work regeneration and faith by a monergistic work of grace? The answer is no. Though the Scriptures clearly teach that God positively decrees the election of some to eternal life from eternity past (Rom. 8:29; Eph. 1:3–14) and actively works in their lives to bring their faith to completion, to those he chose from eternity past *not* to save he withholds his monergistic work of regenerating grace, passing them by and leaving them to themselves (Matt. 11:25–26; Rom. 9:17–18, 21–22; 2 Tim. 2:19–20; 1 Pet. 2:8; Jude 4) to actuate the evil desires of their hearts. That is, God does not monergistically work sin or unbelief in the lives of the reprobate, but instead he leaves them to the ill-deserts of their sin. Thus, while the good in the elect is the direct design of God, evil in the lives of the nonelect is the practical outworking of their own depravity. In summary, although God, of his own good pleasure and will for his glory, from eternity past, equally and ultimately predestines some in Christ to eternal life and others, to eternal destruction, his mode of operation in their lives is different.

This biblical doctrine is a steadfast hallmark of Reformed theology. "None more strongly than Reformed theologians insist that God is not the author of sin. He is not in the same manner (*eodem modo*) the ultimate cause of the death of the lost as he is the ultimate cause of the Salvation of the Saved" (Cornelius Van Til and Eric H. Sigward, *The Works of Cornelius Van Til, 1895–1987*, electronic ed. [New York: Labels Army Co., 1997]). These truths are maintained in many of the historic Reformed creeds, including the *Westminster Confession of Faith*, 3:7; the *Belgic Confession*, article 16; and the *Canons of Dordt*, article 6.

37. Vos, *Biblical Theology*, 141.

Chapter 3: Biblical Preaching: Experiencing the Word of God

1. Tony Evans, *Let's Get to Know Each Other: What White and Black Christians Need to Know about Each Other* (Nashville: Thomas Nelson, 1995), 93. Emphasis added.

2. Cleophus LaRue, "The Heart of Black Preaching," January Lecture Series, Calvin College and Seminary, Grand Rapids, MI, January 27, 2004.

3. Cleophus LaRue, ed., *Power in the Pulpit: How America's Most Effective Black Preachers Prepare Their Sermons* (Louisville, KY: Westminster John Knox Press, 2002), 1.

4. Evans, *Let's Get to Know Each Other*, 90.

5. Anthony J. Carter, *On Being Black and Reformed* (Phillipsburg, NJ: P&R, 2001).

6. Joel Beeke, *Feed My Sheep: A Passionate Plea for Preaching*, ed. Don Kistler (Morgan, PA: Soli Deo Gloria 2002), 95.

7. Ibid., 96.

8. Ibid., 97.

9. Barna and Jackson, *High Impact African-American Churches*, 73.

10. Ibid., 74.

11. Graeme Goldsworthy, *Preaching the Whole Bible as Christian Literature* (Grand Rapids, MI: Eerdmans, 2000), 116.

12. John Calvin, *Institutes of the Christian Religion*, 2.16.19.

13. Terry L. Johnson, *The Case for Traditional Protestantism: The Solas of the Reformation* (Edinburgh: Banner of Truth, 2004), 77.

14. For a concise look at the wonderful doctrine of justification by faith, see John Piper, *Counted Righteous in Christ* (Wheaton, IL: Crossway, 2002). A personal favorite is Horatius Bonar, *The Everlasting Righteousness* (Hobbs, NM: Trinity Foundation, 1994).

15. John Piper, *Brothers, We Are Not Professionals: A Plea to Pastors for Radical Ministry* (Nashville: Broadman and Holman, 2002), 17.

16. Terry L. Johnson, *The Case for Traditional Protestantism: The Solas of the Reformation* (Edinburgh: Banner of Truth, 2004), 102.

17. John Piper, *The Supremacy of God in Preaching* (Grand Rapids, MI: Baker, 1990), 28.

18. Ibid., 20.

Chapter 4: Biblical Worship: Experiencing the Presence of God

1. John Frame, *Worship in Spirit and Truth* (Phillipsburg, NJ: P&R, 1996), 1.

2. Wayne Grudem, *Systematic Theology* (Grand Rapids, MI: Zondervan, 1994), 1003.

3. Philip Ryken, Derek W. H. Thomas, J. Ligon Duncan III, eds. *Give Praise to God: A Vision for Reformed Worship* (Phillipsburg, NJ: P&R, 2003), 61.

4. Louie Giglio, *The Air I Breathe* (Sisters, OR: Multnomah, 2003), 10.

5. "A Purpose Driven Phenomenon: An Interview with Rick Warren," *Modern Reformation*, Jan/Feb, 13, no. 1 (2004): 37–39.

6. The *New International Version* and the *New Living Translation* also translate *abad* in this passage as "worship."

7. D. G. Hart and John R. Muether, *With Reverence and Awe: Returning to the Basics of Reformed Worship* (Phillipsburg, NJ: P&R, 2002), 17.

8. Ibid. Hart and Muether convincingly make this point when they write, "The word *experience* redirects the goal of worship, from God-centeredness to man's pleasure. We become the audience or the consumer, and our criteria for good worship shift," ibid., 17.

9. Robert Darden, *People Get Ready! A New History of Black Gospel Music* (New York: Continuum International, 2004), 197.

10. Ibid., 198.

11. Ibid.

12. The result of this unholy crossover more often than not has been the temporary lucrative success followed by tragic moral failures. Following the tragic life of Rosetta Tharpe were the likes of Clara Ward, Aretha Franklin, Sam Cooke, Al Green, Whitney Houston, and many others.

13. According to John M. Frame, "There are some criteria for good entertainment that are also criteria for God-honoring worship. In worship, sermons should be well-organized and clear, maintaining the attention of the worshippers. Music ought to be of high quality led by skillful (1 Chron. 15:22; 2 Chron. 34:12; Ps. 33:3) artists. It should be memorable, bring its text to dwell in the heart and mind. Those in attendance should feel welcome, among friends. Humor is sometimes valuable in worship, since there is humor in Scripture itself. When these criteria are observed, worship inevitably becomes something like entertainment," *Contemporary Worship Music: A Biblical Defense* (Phillipsburg, NJ: P&R, 1997), 60.

14. Marva Dawn, *How Shall We Worship?* (Wheaton, IL: Tyndale, 2003), 67.

15. George Barna and Harry Jackson Jr., *High Impact African-American Churches: Leadership Concepts from Some of Today's Most Effective Churches* (Ventura, CA: Regal Books, 2004), 102.

16. John Calvin, *Institutes of Christian Religion*, 1.1.

17. Rom. 12:5, 10, 16; 13:8; 14:13, 19; 15:5, 7, 14; 16:16; 1 Cor. 11:33; 12:8, 25; 16:20; 2 Cor. 13:12; Gal. 5:13, 15, 26; Eph. 4:2, 25, 32; 5:19, 21; Col. 3:9, 13, 16; 1 Thess. 3:12; 4:9, 18; 5:11; Heb. 3:13; 10:24–25; James 4:11; 5:9, 16; 1 Pet. 1:22; 3:8; 4:8–10; 5:5, 14; 1 John 1:7; 3:11, 23; 4:11–12; 2 John 1:5.

18. Frame, *Worship in Spirit and Truth*, 77.

19. While it is true that some in the Reformed tradition have advocated downplaying the emotional aspects of worship, preferring to focus upon intellectual comprehension (see Frame, *Worship in Spirit and Truth*, 78), Robert Godfrey rightly sums up what is the correct biblical and Reformed approach when he writes, "A Reformed approach to worship is as much concerned with the heart in worship as with the form of worship. It insists that all true Christians will worship not only with mind and will according to the ordinances of God, but also with godly affection," W. Robert Godfrey, "Worship and the Emotions," in Ryken, Thomas, and Duncan, *Give Praise to God*, 370.

20. Dance in the Scriptures does not seem to be reflective of the modern dance we see prominently in churches today. The texts that mention dance refer to a spontaneous response in worship to God more than a choreographed display. John Frame seems to agree: "I would suggest that in the church 'sacred dance' should be first a spontaneous response to God's blessing. If people want to stand up and move rhythmically to the songs of praise, they should be encouraged to do so. Dance in worship is first of all the simple, natural, physical dimension of the reverent joy we share in Christ" (Frame, *Worship in Spirit and Truth*, 132).

21. The clapping of hands in the Scriptures is reserved for the applause of God (Pss. 47:1; 98:8; Isa. 55:12) or is reflective of mockery and judgment (Lam. 2:15; Ezek. 6:11; 21:14; 21:17; Nah. 3:19). There is also the reference to the anointing of the king and the applause of the people (2 Kings 11:12). Notably missing is the applause for a person's performance in worship.

22. Barna and Jackson, *High Impact African-American Churches*, 87.

23. Frame, *Worship in Spirit and Truth*, 39.

24. *BCF* 22:1; see also *WCF* 21.1.

25. Melva Wilson Costen, *African-American Christian Worship* (Nashville: Abingdon, 1993), 136.

26. Ryken, Thomas, and Duncan, *Give Praise to God*, 65.

27. According to Barna and Jackson, black adults are 50 percent more likely to strongly affirm that the Bible is totally accurate in everything it teaches. *High Impact African-American Churches*, 23.

28. Ryken, Thomas, Duncan, *Give Praise to God*, 66.

29. Costen, *African-American Christian Worship*, 46.

30. See the apostle Paul's admonitions to Timothy concerning the connection between the character of the preacher and the content of his words in 1 Timothy 3:1–7; 6:11–16.

31. Ligon Duncan, "From Worship Wars to Biblical Consensus," Alliance of Confessing Evangelicals, http://www.alliancenet.org/partner/Article_Display_Page/0,,PTID307086%7CCHID559376%7CCIID2046078,00.html.

32. Terry Johnson, *Reformed Worship: Worship That Is According to Scripture* (Greenville, SC: Reformed Academic Press, 2000), 37–38. Quoted in Duncan, "From Worship Wars to Biblical Consensus."

33. Costen, *African-American Christian Worship*, 43.

34. Brenda Aghahowa, *Praising in Black and White: Unity and Diversity in Christian Worship* (Cleveland: United Church Press, 1996), 65, quoted in Barna and Jackson, *High Impact African-American Churches*, 96.

35. Richard Smallwood, "Total Praise" (Brentwood-Benson Music c/o Music Services). Copyright © 1996 Zomba Songs/T Autumn Music.

36. Keith Getty and Stuart Townend, "In Christ Alone" (Thankyou Music [KWY]). Copyright © 2002 Thankyou Music.

37. An excellent treatment of the necessity of psalm singing in our churches today is an essay by Carl R. Trueman entitled "What Can Miserable Christians Sing?" This essay is found in a collection of essays by Trueman, *The Wages of Spin: Critical Writings on Historic and Contemporary Evangelicalism* (Scotland: Mentor Imprint, 2004).

38. Ryken, Thomas, Duncan, *Give Praise to God*, 68.

Chapter 5: Biblical Spirituality: Experiencing the Spirit of God

1. "A New Black Spirituality," *Ebony*, December 2004. http://findarticles.com/p/articles/mi_m1077/is_2_60/ai_n7577964/.

2. Paul K. Conkin, *Puritans & Pragmatists* (New York: Dodd, Mead & Co., 1968), 4.

3. Albert J. Raboteau, *Slave Religion* (New York: Oxford University Press, 1978), 100.

4. Ibid., 100–101.

5. Ibid.

6. Ibid., 73.

7. Patrick Fairbairn, *The Revelation of Law in Scripture* (Lafayette, IN: Sovereign Grace Publishers, 2001).

8. Louis Berkof, *Manual of Christian Doctrine* (Grand Rapids, MI: Eerdmans, 1979), 84.

9. Phillis Wheatley in Henry Louis Gates Jr., *The Trials of Phillis Wheatley* (New York: Basic Civitas Books, 2003), 70–71.

10. Gates, *Trials of Phillis Wheatley*, 71.

11. Ibid., 73–74.

12. Raboteau, *Slave Religion*, 104.

13. Ibid., 107–8.

14. Ibid., 126.

15. Henry Mitchell, *Black Church Beginnings* (Grand Rapids, MI: Eerdmans, 2004), 26.

16. Ibid., 32.

17. Ibid., 24.

18. Melva Wilson Costen, *African American Christian Worship* (Nashville: Abingdon Press, 1993), 37.

19. Dennis L. Okholm, *The Gospel in Black and White: Theological Resources for Racial Reconciliation* (Downers Grove, IL: Intervarsity Press, 1997), 29.

20. Mitchell, *Black Church Beginnings*, 16.

21. Carl F. Ellis, *Free At Last? The Gospel in the African-American Experience* (Downers Grove, IL: InterVarsity, 1996), 47.

22. Juan Williams and Quinton Dixie, *This Far by Faith* (New York: HarperCollins, 2003), 7.

23. Raboteau, *Slave Religion*, 127.

24. W. E. B. DuBois, *The Souls of Black Folk,* ed. Henry Louis Gates Jr. and Terri Hume Oliver (New York: W. W. Norton, 1999), 37.

25. Mitchell, *Black Church Beginnings*, 37.

26. Ibid.

27. Ibid.

28. Raboteau, *Slave Religion*, 132.

29. John Pollock, *George Whitefield and The Great Awakening* (n.p.: Lion Publishing, 1986), 224.

30. Raboteau, *Slave Religion*, 129.

31. Linda E. Thomas, *Living Stones in the Household of God: The Legacy and Future of Black Theology* (Minneapolis: Augsburg Fortress, 2004), 9.

32. Francis Schaeffer, *The Evangelical Disaster* (Wheaton, IL: Crossway, 1984); Mark Noll, David Wells, *God in the Wasteland* (Grand Rapids, MI: Eerdmans, 1994) and *Above All Earthly Powers* (Grand Rapids, MI: Eerdmans, 2005); Michael Horton, *Made in America* (Eugene, OR: Wipf and Stock, 1998); John Armstrong, *The Coming Evangelical Crisis* (Chicago: Moody, 1996).

33. Harold Bloom, *The American Religion* (New York: Simon & Schuster, 1993), 28.

34. Armstrong, *Coming Evangelical Crisis*, 17.

35. James A. Herick, *The Making of the New Spirituality* (Dowers Grove, IL: InterVarsity Press, 2004); Peter Jones, *Spirit Wars* (Mukilteo, WA: Winepress Publishing, 1997).

36. James Montgomery Boice, *Foundations of the Christian Faith: A Comprehensive Biblical Theology* (Downers Grove, IL: InterVarsity Press, 1986), 150.

37. *The Baptist Confession of Faith (1689)*, 6:2.

38. Ibid., 6:4.

39. Ibid., 9:3–4.

40. Berkof, *Manual of Christian Doctrine*, 239.

41. *Baptist Confession*, 16:2.

42. Ibid., 24:1.

43. Ibid., 24:3.

44. Joseph Stump, *An Explanation of Luther's Small Catechism* (St. Louis: Concordia, 1986), 43.

45. Ibid., 49–50.

Chapter 6: Grace So Amazing: Experiencing the Doctrines of Grace

1. John Newton, *The Works of John Newton*, (London: Banner of Truth, 1985), 6:530.

2. Ibid., 522.

3. Steve Turner, *Amazing Grace: The Story of America's Most Beloved Song* (New York: Harper Collins, 2002), 149.

4. Timothy Mather Cooley, *Sketches of the Life and Character of the Rev. Lemuel Haynes, A.M: For Many Years Pastor of a Church in Rutland, Vt., and late in Granville, New-York* (New York: Harper and Brothers, 1837), 28. According to Cooley, Haynes's father was "of unmingled African extraction" (ibid.).

5. John Saillant, *Black Puritan, Black Republican: The Life and Thought of Lemuel Haynes, 1753–1833* (New York: Oxford University Press, 2003), 9.

6. Helen MacLam, "Black Puritan on the Northern Frontier: The Vermont Ministry of Lemuel Haynes," in *Black Preacher to White America: The Collected Writings of Lemuel Haynes, 1774–1883*, ed. by Richard Newman (Brooklyn, NY: Carlson, 1990), xx. Emphasis added.

7. Ibid., xxi.

8. Ibid., xxii.

9. Cooley, *Sketches*, 34.

10. Ibid. Another incident Haynes remembered with terror and gratitude was being chased by an irritated ox who "with his sharp horns inflicted several wounds on his face and head" (ibid.). Haynes was finally able to escape the potentially fatal goring by continually running around a tree until people were able to come and distract the attention of the animal.

11. Ibid.

12. The acronym GRACE is a contemporary expression of the historical doctrines of grace known also as the Five Points of Calvinism. These five points have traditionally been expressed with the acronym TULIP: Total Depravity, Unconditional Election, Limited Atonement, Irresistible Grace, and Perseverance of the Saints.

GRACE is not an improvement upon TULIP, only another way of expressing the glorious biblical truth that salvation is of the Lord, by grace through faith alone.

13. James Montgomery Boice and Phillip Graham Ryken, *The Doctrines of Grace* (Wheaton, IL: Crossway, 2002), 19.

Appendix 1: Sermon Preparation

1. I now write out full manuscripts of my sermons because I receive frequent requests for them.

INDEX

abortion, 137
Adam, 46
affections, 17, 140
African-American church
    and "black preaching," 25, 55–57,
        61–62, 98–99
    and calling to faith, 19–20, 118–22
    and drive for wealth and success,
        11–12
    and evangelicalism, 126–30
    and historic Protestantism, 127,
        150–51
    and influence of revivals, 122–23
    and Reformed theology, 13–19,
        105, 152
    and theology of, 9, 25–30, 44–45,
        59–60, 65
    and sacraments, 103
    worship styles of, 48, 83–87, 94,
        97–105, 128
African Methodist Episcopal Church,
    17
Allen, Richard, 17
American evangelicalism, 25, 28–29,
    108, 122–26
American Indians, 114, 121
Armstrong, John, 126

assurance, 33
atomic exegesis, 48
atonement, 25, 36

baptism, 102, 114
Baptist Confession of Faith, 96, 131,
    133, 136
Barna, George, 10–11, 65, 87, 95, 107
Beeke, Joel, 60–61
Berkeley, George, 109
Berkhof, Louis, 111, 132
Bible
    and creeds and confessions,
        125–26
    as guide to worship, 103
    infallibility of, 38, 48
    inspiration and authority of, 15, 98
    as a literary portrait, 66
    personal study of, 139
    preaching of, 98–99
    public reading of, 97–98
    rejection of, 25
    unity of, 51
    universal truths of and temporal
        conditions, 26–29
    as Word of God, 48–49, 65
    See also inerrancy; regulative

principle of worship; *sola Scriptura.*
biblical commentaries, 156
biblical spirituality, 20, 130–40
biblical theology, 19, 35–36, 64
Bloom, Harold, 125
Boice, James, 130
Brakel, Wilhelmus, 17–18
Bunyan, John, 14
Bynum-Weeks, Juanita, 87

calling
  effectual, 150
  vocational, 55–56, 135–36
Calvin, John, 14, 68, 89, 151
Calvinism, 122, 151–52
Calvinists, 16
Carter, Anthony, 19–20
charismatics, 93
Christian home, 135
Christian worldview, 92
church attendance, 7–10
church fellowship, 91–92
church history, 26–29, 127
Church of England, 109–10
civil government, 137–38
Clowney, Edmund, 38
colonial Christianity, 108–10
communication skills, 57
Cone, James, 123
Congregationalists, 122
Conkin, Paul K., 108
contextualization, 115–18
Cooley, Timothy Mather, 146
Costen, Melva Wilson, 97, 115
covenant families, 135
covenant loyalty, 38, 49
covenant obligations, 52
covenant of grace, 34
Cowper, William, 142–43
creation, 31–33
creation mandate, 135
Creator/creature distinction, 30–31, 34
cultural depravity, 86–87
cultural traditionalism, 129

Dawn, Marva, 86
deacons, 135
death, 71, 131
discipleship, 25
Dixie, Quinton, 117
DuBois, W. F. B., 118
Duncan, Ligon, 80, 97–99, 102

Edwards, Jonathan, 118–20
elders, 135
elect, 72
election, 52, 148–49
Ellis, Carl, 116
emancipation, 109
emotions, 93–94
entertainment, as worship, 85–86
eternity, 52, 69
evangelism, 139
Evans, Tony, 56
evil, 110

Fairbairn, Patrick, 110
faith
  as biblically-grounded, 13–16
  components of, 25
  as experiential, 16–19
  and grace, 72, 132
  persevering in, 52
  saving, 64
  See also sola fide
fall, 43, 46, 131
family values, 75
felt needs, 8–9
financial security, 75
First Great Awakening, 118–22
forgiveness, 45, 67, 90
formalism, 122
Fountain, John, 11–12, 18
Frame, John, 80, 93, 96
freedom, 109, 117

Gates, Henry Louis, 112
Getty, Keith, 101
Gibson, Edmund, 109
Giglio, Louie, 80
glory

eschatological, 43–44
individual, 25
  See also God, glory of
God
  attributes of, 30 (see also
      immanence; transcendence)
  blessings of, 80
  decrees of, 40, 111–12
  desire for, 74
  eternal purposes of, 45–47
  fear of, 94, 160–61
  as focus of worship, 9
  glorifying, 81, 136
  glory of, 21–22, 71, 74, 89 (see also
      soli Deo gloria)
  as infinite and eternal, 32–33
  knowledge of, 29, 65
  sovereignty of, 15, 46–48, 149, 152
  will of, 99
  See also Creator/creature
      distinction; Trinity
Goldsworthy, Graeme, 67–68
good works, 133–34
gospel, 50, 52, 84–85, 138–39, 150
gospel music, 83–84, 100
grace, 52–54, 72, 132, 148–53, 162.
    See also sola gratia
Grudem, Wayne, 80

happiness, 74
Haynes, Lemuel, 146–48
Hebrew language, 155
hedonism, 87
Heidelberg Catechism, 70
hell, 120
Herick, James A., 126
hermeneutic of suspicion, 48
holiness, 43, 52–53, 130
Holy Spirit, 21, 34, 39, 53, 119, 132,
    139–40, 150
Horton, Michael, 125
human accountability, 46–48
hymns, 100–101, 117

immanence, 58–60
incarnation, 39, 63

individualism, 126
inerrancy, 48, 98
intellectualism, 17–18
Israel, 49–52, 81–82, 143

Jackson, Harry, 65, 87, 95, 107
Jakes, T. D., 87
Jesus
  as new covenant head, 132
  and the Old Testament, 39
  person and work of, 25–26, 35–37,
      51, 97 (see also atonement,
      incarnation)
  and preaching, 62–63
  as second Adam, 44
  second coming of, 50
  sufficiency of, 152
  union with, 53, 126, 139
  See also solus Christus; worship, as
      fellowship with Jesus
Johnson, Terry, 72, 99
Jones, Ken, 13, 20
Jones, Peter, 126
joy, 74, 93–94
judgment, 46, 162
justification, 26, 70–71, 132, 134

King, Martin Luther, Jr., 10
kingdom of God, 43, 62–63, 70–71,
    104, 137–39

LaRue, Cleophus, 56, 59
law, 133, 140
Le Jau, Francis, 109, 114
Leach, Michael, 19
Levitical priesthood, 39
Lint, Richard, 29
Lloyd-Jones, D. Martyn, 16
Loggins, Vernon, 120
Long, Eddie, 87
Lord's Supper, 102, 134
Luther, Martin, 13–14, 138–39

Machen, J. Gresham, 72
man
  as created to worship, 92–93
  as image of God, 130

Mather, Cotton, 109–10, 120
Mclaren, Brian, 124
mega-churches, 10–12, 107
mercy, 162
Mitchell, Henry, 113–15, 119–20, 122
Moses, 113

Negro spirituals, 100, 113
neighborly love, 138–39
neo-Pentecostalism, 18
new heavens and earth, 44
"New Lighters," 122
New Testament, worship in, 82
Newton, John, 141–46, 153
Noll, Mark, 125

obedience, 31
Occon, Samson, 112–13
"Old Lighters," 122
Old Testament, worship in, 81–82

pain, 74
Paul, 143
peace, 159–65
peaceful protests, 137
Pentecostalism, 18
personal therapy, 25
personality worship, 87
piety, 122
Piper, John, 71, 76
popular religion, 24
positive thinking, 71, 75
postmodernism, 28
Potter, Ronald, 115
prayer, 80, 99, 121–22
preaching
    and biblical theology, 19, 50–52
    content of, 25, 62–77, 98–99
    and good theology, 57–60
    and the Old Testament, 51–52
    Reformed experiential, 60–62
    with substance, 56–57
    See also African-American church,
        and "black preaching";
        Reformed preachers;

sermons
predestination, 110–12
Presbyterians, 122
Price, Fred, 128
primacy of the intellect, 93
Promised Land, 39
proof-texting, 48
prosperity gospel, 21
Protestantism, 130, 150–51
providence, 110–11, 147–48
Puritanism, 108

Raboteau, Albert, 113–14, 118, 120
reconciliation, 26
redemption, 26, 31–33, 36, 39, 45, 49,
    51, 68, 102, 145, 149–50
redemptive history, 35–44, 51, 143
Reformation, 13–15, 19–20, 108
Reformed preachers, 15–16
Reformed theology, 9, 19, 93
Reformed tradition, 29
Reformers, 21, 75, 135–36
regeneration, 26, 132–33
regulative principle of worship, 96–97
relativism, 95
resurrection, 63
revelation, 35–38
revivalists, 119–20
revivals, 118–23
righteousness, 43, 68–69, 130–31
Roof, Wade Clark, 108
Rose, David, 146

sacraments, 8, 25, 102–3
saints, 104, 150
salvation, 25, 27, 34, 37, 48, 69–73,
    149–50
same-sex marriage, 137
sanctification, 26, 33, 52–54, 68
Schaeffer, Francis, 125
Second Great Awakening, 122–23
secular culture, 23. *See also* cultural
    depravity
self-esteem, 75
seminaries, 57
sermons

declarative, 64
expository, 64
narrative, 64
outlines of, 159–65
preparation of, 155–57
servanthood, 31
Seward, William, 121
sin, 33–35, 46, 69, 82, 92, 94, 120, 123, 131–32, 149, 152, 162
singing, 81, 93, 99–102, 164
slavery, 45–48, 108–18, 142, 145–46
slaves
    and evangelism, 108–10
    and spiritual growth, 115–18
Smallwood, Richard, 101
Society for the Propagation of the Gospel, 110
Society of Negroes, 110
sola fide, 69–72
sola gratia, 72–75
sola Scriptura, 64–67, 96
soli Deo gloria, 75–77
solus Christus, 67–69
sorrow, 74, 94
spiritual formation, 134
spiritual gifts, 134
spiritual realities, 88
subjective experience, 18, 122
submission, 101, 137
syncretism, 24

tabernacle, 39
Taylor, Ebenezer, 113–14
temple, 39
temporal prosperity, 25
temptation, 52
Tharpe, Rosetta, 83–84
theology
    and black spirituality, 123–26
    definition of, 30–35
    orthodox, 122
    See also biblical theology;
        Reformed theology
Thomas, Linda E., 123
total depravity, 131, 149
Townsend, Stuart, 101

transcendence, 58, 60
Trinity, 25
truth
    experiencing, 76, 130
    objective, 18
    standard of, 25, 48
Tubman, Harriet, 113
Turner, Steve, 145

Underground Railroad, 113
universe, restoration of, 38–44

Warren, Rick, 81
wealth, 71
Wells, David, 125
Wesley, John, 120–21
Westminster Confession of Faith, 30–31, 34
Westminster Shorter Catechism, 81
Wheatley, Phillis, 112–13
Whitefield, George, 119–21
whooping, 61
Wilberforce, William, 144
Williams, Juan, 117
wisdom literature, 39
women clergy, 107
world, 76, 84–85
worldliness, 23–24
worship
    biblical, 92–103
    and biblical theology, 49–50
    contemporary style of, 100, 104
    corporate, 134
    definition of, 80–88
    as fellowship with Jesus, 90–92
    form and content of, 20 (see also regulative principle of worship)
    human-centered, 25
    as meeting with God, 88–90
    orders of, 167–71
    physical expression in, 95
    in slave communities, 117–18
    traditional style of, 100, 104
wrath, 72